THE FABULOUS FRUCTOSE RECIPE BOOK

THE FABULOUS FRUCTOSE RECIPE BOOK

by J. T. Cooper, M. D.

and Jeanne Jones

M. EVANS AND COMPANY, INC. · *New York*

Library of Congress Cataloging in Publication Data

Cooper, James Thomas, 1935–
   The fabulous fructose recipe book.

   Bibliography: p.
   Includes index.
   1. Sucrose-free diet—Recipes. 2. Cookery
(Fructose) I. Jones, Jeanne, joint author.
II. Title.
RM237.85.C66   641.5'635   79-18221
ISBN 0-87131-304-9

M. Evans and Company, Inc.
216 East 49 Street
New York, New York 10017

Design by Ronald F. Shey

Manufactured in the United States of America

9 8 7 6 5 4 3 2 1

C 2

To all of the Fabulous Bears everywhere

In grateful acknowledgment:
Joy Kirkpatrick, R.D., for technical advice and
professional assistance

Contents

PART ONE: BACKGROUND   1
Introduction   *13*
The Fabulous Fructose Diet   *16*
The Fabulous Fructose Seven-Day Maintenance
    Diet   *21*
What Happens When Your Weight Goes Up?   *28*
Questions and Answers   *34*

PART TWO: COOKING   37
Introduction   *39*
Stocks and Soups   *41*
Sauces and Salad Dressings   *62*
Salads   *84*
Vegetables and Grains   *100*
Eggs and Cheese Dishes   *113*
Fish and Shellfish   *128*
Poultry   *138*
Meat   *148*
Breads   *157*
Desserts and Dessert Sauces   *174*
Beverages   *203*

CONTENTS

APPENDIXES 211

1 Food Lists *213*
2 Basal Caloric Needs *241*
3 Advice on Buying Fructose Products *242*
4 Suppliers and Information Sources *243*
5 Beware the Feeder *246*
6 An Open Letter to the Spouse (or Parent or Friend) of
  My Patients *249*

BIBLIOGRAPHY 253

INDEX 255

PART ONE

BACKGROUND

Introduction

With the publication of *Dr. Cooper's Fabulous Fructose Diet* a new era in weight reduction has begun. This exciting and innovative method of weight reduction has had a success record that is nothing short of phenomenal. The average problem dieter has at last found a rapid and relatively painless but still safe diet program in the Fabulous Fructose Diet.

Patients who never had been able to lose significant amounts of weight are shedding pounds and singing the praises of properly utilized fructose feedings as part of their daily food intake. Literally millions of pounds have been shed by the followers of the different fructose diets outlined in my first book.

Criticisms also began to come in about the FFD. The most common ones were that the initial two-week priming diet was too high in cholesterol and sodium, and that there was too little variety in the recipes and meal plans given. There was a relative absence of gourmet recipes in Appendix 5 of the book. I feel these are valid criticisms and that, indeed, it is difficult to stay on a weight reduction or weight maintenance program if one is bored or jaded with the regime given.

When I looked over almost all the other diet books published in the past ten years, either by doctors or by lay authors, I found the same problem. The problem is what to do after the desired weight is attained. Average dieters are prone at this point to fall victim to the "Ah-Hah Phenomenon." They get to their weight goal and say, "Ah-Hah! I have lost all my weight and I am cured. I can now eat all I want again."

3

This attitude is the downfall of 95 percent or more of the dieters who reach their goal. They rapidly or gradually regain the weight they have lost and even more when they resume old faulty eating habits. The purpose of this book is to make sure that people who have been on the Fabulous Fructose Diet, *or any other diet,* can not only maintain their desired weight, but can do it in a comfortable manner without the fear of regaining the excess pounds that have plagued them in the past.

This book will also make recipes available to you that will be tasty and practical, prudent in cholesterol and sodium content, and usable by the homemaker with lots of time as well as by the worker with the need for something easy to prepare. The recipes can be used both by diabetics and by people with heart disease.

For those who wish fiber content to be listed, we have information in Appendix 1 about its content in different foods and recipes. The fiber content will not be a major concern, but it is provided for your information. There is still a lot of debate in the medical and lay press about fiber, and this book will not address itself directly to the controversy. The best course for you if this interests you, and you wish higher fiber content, is to consult your physician for definitive guidance in the amounts of fiber, cholesterol, fat and sodium that you should take in daily. Only your personal physician knows your condition well enough to make these decisions and you should consult with him or her before going on *any* program of weight reduction or maintenance.

If you or your doctor need additional information or wish to obtain the name and address of a bariatrician (a physician specializing in weight control) in your area, you may write to the American Society for Bariatric Physicians, 5200 South Quebec Street, Englewood, Colorado, or call 303-779-4833.

I consider myself quite fortunate in having as my coauthor Jeanne Jones, author of many excellent books on diet and nutrition (see the Bibliography). She is a contributor to many medically oriented publications, a superb gourmet cook, an internationally recognized hostess and a walking encyclopedia of nutrition.

Between the two of us, we promise you an interesting, exciting and effective program in the art and science of diet cookery and meal planning. We could have subtitled this book, *The Rest of Your Life Cookbook*, or *Life After Weight Loss*. To you who are reading this book, we say, "Enjoy!"

J. T. Cooper, M.D.

The Fabulous Fructose Diet

In my first book, *Dr. Cooper's Fabulous Fructose Diet,* the reasons for failure in most diets were discussed. Briefly, many people are unable to stay on a weight reduction diet because of a built-in failure factor, the Glucose-Insulin Trap. The constant consumption of foods high in refined sucrose and glucose sets up a mechanism that results in rapid upward surges in the level of blood glucose, followed by episodes of low blood glucose, followed each time by an all-consuming hunger that drives the dieter back to more sugar, etc. This up-and-down, roller-coaster effect causes a constant intake of sugar and readily digested starches all day long and this results in an almost pathological and continuous weight gain. For full details, see the appropriate sections in this book. There are detailed explanations and charts.

I would also suggest you look at the Appendixes of the fructose diet book. I have mentioned there several criteria for determining whether or not you have hypoglycemia or what I call pseudohypoglycemia. They are my criteria and are open to criticism or disagreement by some of my colleagues, but it should be pointed out here that the only thing two physicians can agree on is how much charity work a third doctor should do.

The remedy for this Glucose-Insulin Trap would seem to be obvious: omit all sugars and starches and only eat meats and salads. This works for some patients for a relatively short time,

6

but many times, even in ketosis, the patient would be taking in massive amounts of meat and fat and exceeding the energy needs for the day, resulting in a weight gain instead of a loss. The high fat intake, with some meats having thirty percent or more fat content, is not ideal for patients already susceptible to arteriosclerosis. Not only that, but the patients on this low carbohydrate diet would invariably feel rotten and washed out, and would have what one of my Oriental patients calls "Dragon Breath."

By adding small amounts of fructose to the daily diet and by limiting the quantity of protein and calories taken in each day to a reasonable amount, we were able to achieve the best of both worlds. We had little if any ketosis, and the caloric intake was low enough to produce a significant deficit and a noticeable weight loss without the feeling of being washed out and tired all the time.

Many of my professional colleagues and friends pointed out to me that there were obvious flaws in the Fabulous Fructose Diet of which I was already aware. In brief, there was not enough flexibility in the FFD as presented in the first book. Patients with special needs for low sodium, low cholesterol, high fiber, and others, were not able comfortably to use the diet in its present form. There were not enough recipes for interesting food, both for the cook who starts from scratch and for the working person who must sometimes prepare a meal in a short time.

I was also aware that the initial, fourteen-day priming diet was rather high in cholesterol, saturated fats and sodium. My reasoning for using this diet initially for most patients was that this probably wasn't too different in content from their accustomed diet, except that the carbohydrate content had been dropped drastically. After the fourteen-day priming diet, the other four diet plans mentioned in the FFD will be found to be relatively low in fats, refined sugars and cholesterol.

I have also noted that a diet like this, of two weeks or less, will not really affect the patient on a long-term basis and there-

7

fore does much more good in weight reduction than it could possibly do harm in temporary excesses of sodium or cholesterol.

There have been many studies that have questioned whether or not eggs and similar "high-cholesterol" foods were the villains in arteriosclerosis. The long-term effects of these differences in dietary intake are still in question, but to satisfy anyone who might be concerned about the content of these substances in a weight reduction or maintenance program, we have included provisions for diets low in cholesterol and sodium.

WHAT DO I DO NOW?

The most common time of failure for a dieter who has lost the required amount of weight is during the weight maintenance phase. Unless a strong hand is used at this phase to make sure that the patient doesn't get out of hand, the weight is gradually or rapidly regained and another failure occurs. This should never be allowed to happen. In order to make sure that the graduates of any weight reduction diet, either the FFD or others, do not fall into this trap, we have an entire program of dietary management, psychological support and exercise suggestions. Upon the foundation of these three different but interlocking principles rests the key to permanent and happy slimness.

The first thing you should do is to review the principles of avoiding any environmental influences that might trigger your eating in a problematic way. The most common problems in the environment have to do with what I call Feeders and with the family or close friend who knowingly or unwittingly causes you to go off your diet. Since your protection from these two influences is so important, I am reprinting two warning sheets from my fructose diet book, "Beware the Feeder" and "An Open Letter to the Spouse (or Parent or Friend), of My Patients," in Appendixes 5 and 6 of the book. Make sure you are immune to the feeders and that your spouse or those closest to you read about what they need to do to help you.

It is amazing how many of the people you think of as friends will try to get you to go off your diet and, failing that, will try to get you to regain your weight after you have succeeded in reaching a slim figure. Be polite but firm in your assertiveness and don't let them get to you. In the event you don't have anyone like this in your family or circle of friends, consider yourself blessed.

The second thing needed to lose and maintain your weight loss is to keep your activity high. Walking, swimming, cycling or other aerobic exercises are excellent. For a full treatment of what Dr. Kenneth Cooper calls aerobics, see one of several of his many publications on the subject. A number of Dr. Cooper's books are listed in the Bibliography.

The last factor to consider in long-term weight-loss maintenance is the continuance of a caloric intake that is balanced with caloric output. It is obvious that no person either eats the same amount of food or burns the same amount of energy every day. The usual thing to do is to calculate your approximate caloric needs (see Appendix 2) and try to limit your caloric intake accordingly. At the end of the week you should not have gained or lost more than a few ounces or the intake is off.

What most people fail to realize is that the exchange or portion method of calculating the calories, fat, protein and carbohydrate of a portion of food is only approximately correct and exact. An example would be a fruit exchange. If one takes a dozen apples of about two inches in diameter and *really* analyzes how many calories are available to our bodies from eating each one, we will obtain twelve different readings with an average of about 10 grams carbohydrate or 40 calories per apple. None will be exactly this amount perhaps, but the average amount will be very close to it. With all the other foods on a portion or exchange program there will be the same limitations as to determining their exact content of calories and grams of the different types of nutrients.

9

This means that, for example, to get exactly 1700 calories a day, every day, is impossible, but the averages should cancel out the effects of the portions either lower or higher than their book values. Another factor making things difficult is the relatively large fluctuations in physical activity from day to day, thus again affecting our caloric balance. A daily routine of exercise that is pretty close to constant would help eliminate a lot of the discrepancies and help the dieter hold at a certain weight a lot more easily.

The thing that helps this book to help you is its versatility and flexibility in dealing with what you take in as food every day. Using this program as described on the following pages you can maintain your weight after ANY diet and not just the FFD.

For the first time, to our knowledge, we have in a cookbook a list of most of the foods used in American diets, along with the calories, diabetic exchange data, cholesterol content, sodium and fiber contents. All recipes are also broken down into the various dietary factors to provide maximum nutritional information for the dietician, the physician and the patient.

In the event there is a temporary gain of non-water weight that can be credited to actual fat gain, there is also a seven-day Emergency Diet to help bring the weight down to the desired mark. The Emergency Diet can be used in a number of ways, as a priming diet to take off weight and as a periodic slim-down for persons who occasionally are trapped into excess eating by holidays, weddings, family gatherings and other situations where control slips away from them.

Returning to your daily caloric needs, there is an average caloric need for each day for everyone. This can change as a person ages, goes through stress (pregnancy, surgery, illness, or work- or home-related problems), changes physical activity and other habits. The caloric needs do vary from day to day, but over a week there is an averaging effect. The bottom line in any calculation of this sort is whether the person loses, gains or maintains his weight over a prolonged period of time. A person with a caloric need of 1700 will gain if he takes in 1800 and lose if he consumes 1600 calories daily over a period of time.

Even small fluctuations can cause problems over a prolonged period. If you were to take in only 10 calories a day more than you used, in a year you would have accumulated 3650 calories extra, almost exactly the amount of calories in a pound of body fat.

Use this book as a companion volume to *Dr. Cooper's Fabulous Fructose Diet* and together they should help you not only to lose weight, but to keep it off in a healthy, tasty and interesting way. At a risk of too much repetition, review the chapters of the first book that deal with your own mental attitudes and your environment. Review again the reasons for using fructose as an integral and permanent part of your daily food intake. Try to master completely the explanation of the glucose-insulin trap and know which foods and beverages worsen it and which ones do not. That is the key to success in dieting.

PORTIONS, SHARES AND EXCHANGES

A long time ago it became obvious to many diabetologists that unless the proper balance of nutrients taken in by the body was obtained, there would be a poorer control of diabetes and shorter lives for those affected. It also was obvious that the average diabetic did not have analytical scales and the ability to measure in minute amounts the foods and other nutrients consumed every day. In order to insure at least minimal adherence to a diabetic diet the exchange system was developed. It has undergone a number of changes in the past decades, but the basic principles remain valid.

It was discovered that within certain food groups there is an approximate equivalence of the C-P-F (Carbohydrate-Protein-Fat) ratios. This means that a certain amount of a food type is equivalent in its C-P-F to a certain amount of a similar food.

By careful analysis these ratios were determined and the quantities of each food in a group were standardized to equal each other.

Using the fruit group as an example again, the amounts of C-P-F in a small apple, half a cup of blackberries and 2 medium apricots are all about the same—10 grams of carbohydrate. This means that the C-P-F for all these is 10-0-0 and each portion, of almost pure carbohydrate content, has 40 calories.

The word "exchange" seems to confuse a lot of patients, and many other words have been used for the same purpose. Instead of exchange, substitute the words "share," "portion," or "unit." Most patients have heard of or used the word "portion" more than any other word, so we will use portions as the units of measure in determining food quantities. A portion of food may mean different things to different people, but here portion has a special meaning. It refers to the amount of food based on its essential nutritional content (protein, carbohydrates, fats) rather than on the volume or weight of the food. One small correction in this book versus the fructose diet book is the use of the protein share in the latter. A protein share in the earlier diet book is equivalent to two average protein portions in this book, but in this book we have actually used three different types of protein portion, low-fat, medium-fat and high-fat portions, each with a different C-P-F ratio. We will discuss this in the next section of this chapter.

It is almost universally agreed that a certain protein intake must be maintained each day in order to keep the person on a diet in a healthy state. It is also almost completely agreed on, that the type of carbohydrate consumed should be either of the starchy or the slowly absorbed kind, and that rapidly absorbed sugars should be absent or in minimal quantities in the daily diet. This means that potatoes, bread and fruit would be alright, but sucrose (table sugar) and other rapidly absorbed simple sugars (glucose, dextrose and galactose) would be forbidden. Fortunately, fructose *is* absorbed slowly and can be used in our diets.

The disagreements come in the percentage of the total calories derived from carbohydrate and in the percentage of the daily intake devoted to fat, with the ratios of saturated and unsaturated fat also bones of contention. These disagreements are between groups of excellent clinicians who are all honestly trying to help keep their diabetic and/or obese patients controlled by diet. Each believes that his theory is correct and it would be presumptious of me to dispute such learned men and women. For the purposes of this cookbook and to make things easy for the average person trying, with his doctor's help, to follow our directions, we are going to go by the present official standards of the American Diabetes Association and the American Dietetic Association. If your doctor feels that a different "mix" of foods is needed, go by his advice since it comes from the doctor who knows your condition and needs better than any one else.

Now I will discuss the different kinds of food portions, following the order of the food portion lists in Appendix 1 of this book. You may want to look at the lists as you read.

FRUIT PORTIONS

Most of the foods that fall into the fruit category, namely with a C-P-F of 10-0-0, are indeed fruits, but some are sugar-based foods like molasses or sucrose (table sugar), or honey. While the latter three are put into the list (see Appendix 1) for information purposes, they should be avoided on diabetic diets and reduction regimes as being counterproductive and the proper amount of fructose substituted in their place in recipes.

It is always best to have fresh fruits, but unsweetened juices and fruits that are fresh-frozen or canned in water are also acceptable. If the label says either "sweetened," "packed in heavy syrup," or "packed in light syrup," do not eat it. The amount of refined sugar in these foods is too much and it will ruin your diet. The very word "syrup" means sugar in all cases and is your clue that the food is undesirable. The one exception is any product that has fructose in syrup form and no other sugars along with it. A 90 percent fructose syrup (fructose-90) is permitted.

13

At the writing of this book I have just tasted a honey-flavored fructose syrup that is indistinguishable from honey, with 90 percent fructose instead of the usual 40 percent found in regular honey. There will also be fructose-sweetened jams, preserves, jellies, candies, mints and other confections available in most grocery and health-food stores and by mail order before this book is published. This brings up a need for caution. Always figure the amount of fructose in grams in each of these along with any fruit carbohydrate content (usually on the jar or package); for every 10 grams of fructose or fruit content, subtract one fruit portion from that day's food intake. If you are using the fructose diet book's maintenance diet, subtract the number of grams of fructose and fruit taken in from the day's ration for each of these on the tables provided. *Never exceed the daily recommendations for fruit portions and fructose; this could cause problems in diabetic and/or weight control!*

You will notice that there is a wide variety of fruits, berries, juices and other foods on the list. Those with good content of vitamin C and vitamin A are marked, with some having both in respectable amounts. As in all foods listed in this and subsequent lists, we have listed the fiber, cholesterol and sodium content for your information.

VEGETABLE PORTIONS

The foods in this category have a C-P-F of 5-2-0. They are basically foods of vegetable origin that are mostly carbohydrate with a small amount of protein, and little or no fat. They are not all what most of us think of as vegetables. Those not included in this group have a much higher carbohydrate content and are handled by the body as if they were almost pure starch with a small amount of protein. This is an important thing to realize, that "vegetables" come in two forms and there *is* a difference.

Many of my patients who come back with a weight gain say that they are being very careful and are eating lots of vegetables. When we analyze which ones, there are a lot of beans, potatoes, corn and similar starchy vegetables that are more breadlike than saladlike. Because it is such a problem, please study both the vegetable portion list and the vegetables listed in the starch portion list in Appendix 1 and try to learn the differences between the two apparently similar but actually quite different groups of foods.

In the vegetable portions there is a lot of cellulose and fibrous material that gives bulk but cannot be absorbed in its natural state. For many of these there is virtually no absorbable food value when eaten raw; these are marked as such. You may eat as much of this group as you want if it is uncooked. If this same food is cooked, the heat of cooking breaks down the cellulose molecules to smaller fragments that can be absorbed partially by the intestinal tract and we can then realize food value from the food. The cooked form then must be figured into our daily needs, whereas the raw form could be eaten in generous quantities without adding many calories at all to the daily intake.

There are certain foods included that are not vegetables, but are derived from vegetables. Tomato catsup, tomato paste and tomato sauce are good examples of this, and you must be careful with these. The dietetic catsup has only 6 milligrams sodium per portion compared to regular catsup with about 282 milligrams. On a low-sodium diet it would be easy to stray away from the diet prescription with regular catsup; for that reason it pays to read labels and charts for your own protection.

No matter what the fiber content, sodium content or form, the total calories per serving are 25, with protein making up from 20 to 25 percent of the total. You will again notice the content of vitamins C and A listed for your information.

STARCH (BREADLIKE) PORTIONS

Now we get into what is possibly the greatest area of temptation for the dieter and a food group that is grossly misunderstood. On a maintenance diet it is important that a certain amount of the food intake be in the form of these foods. The C-P-F for the starch portion is 15-2-0. There is three times as much carbohydrate per starch portion as with the vegetable portion, but the protein is the same. There is again almost no fat, and the calories per portion are 70.

In the list in Appendix 1 we have broken the starches down into starchy vegetables, breads, cereals, flours, crackers, and miscellaneous, and we will cover each one briefly. Most of the starchy vegetables are derived from seed or root sources. This means that the beans, corn, rice, parsnips and potatoes listed are storage forms of energy and are used by the plant for future energy, as with the potato, or for propagation of new plants, as with corn kernels. The relatively small amount of protein present is for the biochemical "machinery" necessary for future energy production or for continuation of the plant species.

Whether or not the foods mentioned under starch portions are cooked, the food value is roughly the same. This is another difference between this group and the true "vegetables" from the previous list. Other processed foods such as potato chips are listed for information purposes, but look at the higher sodium content in these foods!

You will notice, under breads, that tremendous amounts of baked products are listed. These make ideal vehicles for the use of fructose-containing foods like the jams, syrups, etc., mentioned on previous pages. There is absolutely no reason why you couldn't have an English muffin with fructose jam, or two pancakes with fructose "honey" on top, or a slice of whole-grain toast with a generous portion of fructose orange marmalade. You will have to calculate each part of the food intake, but this becomes automatic after a while and certainly makes things a lot more pleasant on your diet regime.

While a lot of different breads are mentioned, and at the risk of sounding like a "food nut," it is a good idea to use whole-grain breads where possible. The taste and texture is usually better and the extra nutrients are worth the trouble of selecting this type of bread. You can, however, use any of these breads interchangeably and get the same amount of calories, protein and carbohydrate.

Cereals are the bane of the dieter. If one is not careful in selection of a good cereal product, there may be more sugar purchased than cereal. There are many grains used in cereal preparation, with wheat, rice, oats and corn being some that are used. Avoid those with sugar frosting and flavoring. Remember that for many of these cereals you are better off eating the cardboard carton than you are consuming the contents! The bran listed in several places is good sprinkled over cereal, mixed with unflavored yogurt and fructose-sweetened preserves, or baked in muffins. If you want or need a lot of fiber, this is one of the best and most economical ways to get it.

The lists of flours, crackers and some miscellaneous items are provided for information in cooking and for use in determining the value of certain snack foods. It is obvious that you could soon exceed your sodium allowance for the day if these snack crackers are eaten in any great amount, not to mention the caloric overkill. During the average weight reduction diet it is well to stay away from this type of food and reserve it for the maintenance phase of your program.

LOW-FAT PROTEIN PORTIONS

In this category of protein foods and in the next two categories, each with a slightly higher fat and caloric content per portion, are some foods that are not traditionally thought of as protein by many people, but have the same C-P-F ratio in each category as meat. The three groups all have 7 grams of protein per portion, but vary in their fat content. The low-fat group has a C-P-F ratio of 0-7-3 and a caloric content of 55 calories per portion. There is probably a small but significant amount of carbohydrate in some foods of the group, but we can safely ignore this for purposes of calculating a reduction or maintenance diet. These are the more desirable proteins, with fish making up a large portion of the group's selections.

MEDIUM-FAT PROTEIN PORTIONS

This next group is somewhat higher in fat with a ratio of 0-7-5 and a caloric content of about 75 per portion. It is a good idea to study the cholesterol and sodium content of this group and the next, high-fat protein group, in order to stay within the bounds of your diet if such substances are restricted.

HIGH-FAT PROTEIN PORTIONS

This highest-in-fat-content group has a C-P-F of 0-7-7 with each portion containing about 95 calories. It is much less desirable and should make up a relatively small part of your weekly protein intake. This group includes things such as peanut butter, cold cuts and canned sausages or Spam. A good rule of thumb is to have none of these more than once a week each.

FAT PORTIONS

There are many things that we wouldn't normally classify as fat, but they are, indeed, almost pure fat. Nobody would mistake butter or margarine for anything else but fat, but olives, avocados, bacon, nuts and salad dressings are sometimes confused by the dieter and put into another group by mistake. A classic example would be mistaking bacon for a meat, or avocado for a fruit. The C-P-F of fat portions is 0-0-5 with each portion containing 45 calories.

NONFAT MILK PORTIONS

The nonfat milk portions include various products, with many having a respectable amount of sodium. One should especially watch the buttermilk for its sodium content. Yogurt and sherbet must also be watched for unwanted sucrose content. One favorite tactic of some of the yogurt producers in this country is to label their products as low in fat, but conveniently to forget to tell the unsuspecting buyer that the products, both regular and frozen yogurt, are loaded with sugar. When I wrote one company and asked if they would substitute fructose for the less desirable sucrose, they politely told me to mind my own business. Perhaps if enough people bought a brand that either had no sugar or only had fructose in the flavored kinds, maybe these companies would see the light and change their formulas. In the meantime, read all labels and avoid any frozen yogurt that doesn't have fructose as the *only* sugar present.

LOW-FAT MILK PORTIONS

This group has a C-P-F of 12-8-5 and a caloric content of 125 per portion, compared with 12-8-0 and 80 calories in the nonfat group. Again, the infamous sweetened flavored yogurt is in this group, so watch out!

WHOLE MILK PORTIONS

This last group has the highest fat content of all and a ratio of 12-8-10 with 170 calories per portion. Watch the ice milk as a source of hidden and unwanted sugar. Incidentally, when I say sugar I am speaking of sucrose or dextrose (glucose) and am not referring to fructose.

HERBS, SPICES, SEASONINGS, ETC.

This entire group has negligible calories and can be used as condiment or filler in recipes. Watch the sodium content carefully if sodium restriction has been advised. Many of these are loaded with sodium and should be used sparingly.

ALCOHOLIC BEVERAGES

When any of these is used in cooking, most of the alcohol is evaporated off before consumption and the calories remaining are negligible. Where alcohol is taken in as a beverage the body metabolizes the alcohol in the drink as if it were a fat. A lot of distilled spirits have almost no carbohydrate content at all and can be considered to be used by the body as fat. When wine is drunk it is important to use one with lesser amounts of carbohydrates. An example is a 3-ounce glass of sweet Marsala with 18 grams carbohydrate and 158 total calories, contrasted with the same amount of dry white wine having under 1 gram of carbohydrate and only 74 calories, less than half as much food energy.

In *Dr. Cooper's Fabulous Fructose Diet* we also have compared the food value of different alcoholic beverages. A look at the table in the diet book (pp. 159–160) will also be an eye opener. One thing that is rarely understood about alcohol is its ability to sabotage the weight loss and maintenance programs in three ways. It tends to suppress fat mobilization, it stimulates fat production, and it acts through the stimulation of the glucose-insulin trap indirectly to produce an irresistible hunger in susceptible persons.

A final word to the wise: Stay away from alcohol while you are trying to lose weight unless you are closely followed by your physician, and use alcohol with a lot of restraint and moderation after you are at your maintenance weight.

The Fabulous Fructose Seven-Day Maintenance Diet

The Fabulous Fructose Seven-Day Maintenance Diet is designed to give you a perfectly balanced diet program between 1200 and 1500 calories per day, and it is balanced nutritionally to give you the right number of portions of each food necessary for good health each day. If you wish *to lower the amounts of cholesterol* in your diet, apply the following restrictions to your program:

1. Limit or avoid egg yolks, substituting liquid egg substitute, low in cholesterol, for them.
2. Limit shellfish such as oysters, clams, scallops, lobsters, shrimps and crabs.
3. Limit or avoid organ meats of all animals, such as liver, heart, kidney, sweetbreads and brains.

To lower the amount of saturated fat in your diet, apply the following rules:

1. Use liquid vegetable oils and margarines that are high in polyunsaturated fats instead of butter. Two of the best oils for this purpose are safflower oil and corn oil.
2. Do not use coconut oil or chocolate. Many nondairy creamers and sour-cream substitutes contain coconut oil. Use coconut extract and dry powdered cocoa or carob powder.

3. Use nonfat milk, or low-sodium low-fat milk if on a low-sodium diet.
4. Avoid commercial ice cream.
5. Limit the amount of beef, lamb, and pork in your diet to four or five times a week and eat fish, chicken, veal and white meat of turkey in their place.
6. Buy lean cuts of meat and trim all visible fat from them before cooking.

To lower sodium in your diet, eliminate the use of ordinary table salt, soy sauce and all condiments high in sodium. If it is necessary to lower the sodium greatly, check the amounts of sodium in all foods you are using in the food lists in Appendix 1. For example, you will find that you can greatly reduce sodium by using nothing but low-sodium milk and unsalted corn oil margarine.

Following the Fabulous Fructose Seven-Day Maintenance Diet program is the Emergency Diet plan. This is also a perfectly balanced diet for only 800 calories per day. It is designed to help you through the times when you find you are putting on a few extra unwanted pounds and wish to get back to a permanent plateau. Some of the recipes suggested for these diets are found in Part Two. Check the index to locate them.

Before going on this or any other diet program, always check with your own doctor.

THE FABULOUS FRUCTOSE MAINTENANCE DIET PROGRAM

2 quarts of water throughout the day
2-gram (8-calorie) fructose tablets as needed (not to exceed 10)

BREAKFAST
1 fruit portion
2 low- or medium-fat protein portions
1 starch portion
3 fat portions
1 nonfat milk portion*

LUNCH
3 low- or medium-fat protein portions
1 or 2 starch portions
2 fat portions
1 or 2 vegetable portions
1 or 2 fruit portions
½ nonfat milk portion
Free food as desired

DINNER
3 or 4 low- or medium-fat protein portions
1 starch portion
2 fat portions
1 vegetable portion
1 fruit portion
½ nonfat milk portion
Free foods as desired

I routinely use nonfat milk, which allows more leeway with fat portions. If you use low-fat milk, subtract 1 fat allowed for the meal. If you use whole milk, subtract 2 fats. Fat portions may be saved up from one meal to another and used to have more salad dressing on a salad or more corn oil margarine on a slice of toast.

SEVEN-DAY FABULOUS FRUCTOSE MAINTENANCE DIET MENUS

DAY ONE

BREAKFAST
½ cup fresh orange juice
1 soft-boiled egg, or ½ cup liquid egg substitute
3 slices of Canyon Ranch Bread
2 teaspoons corn oil margarine
1 cup nonfat milk

LUNCH
1 serving Soufflé-Textured Tuna Aspic
1 Show-Off Popover
½ cup unsweetened pineapple
1 cup nonfat milk

DINNER
1 serving Strawberry Soup
3 portions roast turkey without skin
1 serving Mashed Potato Spoof
1 serving Herbed Vegetable Medley
1 serving Creamy Cheese Pie

DAY TWO

BREAKFAST
½ cup low-fat cottage cheese
½ cup Popular Porridge
1 cup nonfat milk

LUNCH
Tossed green salad with 2 tablespoons Fabulous Dressing
1½ servings Pizza Chicken
1 serving Zucchini in Herb Butter
1 slice of crusty Italian bread
½ cup sliced fresh peaches with 2 tablespoons "Amaretto" Sauce
½ cup nonfat milk

DINNER
½ serving Dilled Cucumbers
4 ounces poached salmon with ¼ cup Dilled Yogurt Dressing
1 slice of Lettuce Bread
1 tomato, sliced
1 serving Cold Banana Soufflé with 2 tablespoons Caribbean
   Rum Sauce

DAY THREE

BREAKFAST
¼ cantaloupe
2 ounces Monterey Jack cheese melted on ½ English muffin
1 cup nonfat milk

LUNCH
1 cup Calcutta Consommé
1 serving Szechuan Shrimp Salad
1 Pineapple Muffin
1 serving Rhubarb Compote with ½ cup plain low-fat yogurt

DINNER
1 serving Stracciatella alla Romana
1 cup cold steamed zucchini with 2 tablespoons Fabulous Dressing
1 serving Fabulous Stew
1 serving Strawberries Hoffmann-La Roche over ¼ cup low-fat
   cottage cheese

DAY FOUR

BREAKFAST
1 banana sliced on 1½ cups puffed rice cereal with 1 cup nonfat
  milk
¼ cup low-fat cottage cheese

LUNCH
1 serving Minestrone
1 serving Apple and Cheese Salad
1 slice of Canyon Ranch Bread
1 cup nonfat milk

DINNER
1 serving Tabbouli (Lebanese Salad)
1 serving Turkish Turkey
1 serving Zucchini in Herb Butter
1 serving Lavash
1 serving Peanut Butter Pie

DAY FIVE

BREAKFAST
1 serving Date Nut Waffle with 1 teaspoon corn oil margarine
1 serving Dieter's Spicy Sausage
1 cup nonfat milk

LUNCH
1½ servings Carrots à l'Indienne
1 slice of Banana Bread
½ cup unsweetened pineapple with 2 tablespoons "Coconut"
  Sauce
1 cup nonfat milk

DINNER
1 serving Gazpacho with 6 Toasted Tortilla Triangles
6 ounces poached or baked fresh fish
1 serving Ravable Rice
½ fresh papaya with lime

DAY SIX

BREAKFAST
½ grapefruit
2 servings English Pizza
1 cup nonfat milk

LUNCH
1 serving Curried Carrot Salad
1 serving Eggs Foo Yung
1 serving South Seas Pineapple Pie
1 cup nonfat milk

DINNER
1 serving tossed green salad with 2 tablespoons Skinny Dressing
1½ servings Fabulous Stew
1 serving English Trifle

DAY SEVEN

BREAKFAST
1 serving San Francisco Sourdough French Toast with ½ cup
  Strawberry Jam
1 cup nonfat milk

LUNCH
1 serving Cold Consommé with Mushrooms
1 serving Fabulous Curried Chicken Salad in Lettuce Bowls
1 slice of Orange Rye Bread
1 serving rum-flavored Jelled Water

DINNER
1 sliced tomato with 2 tablespoons Mystery Dressing
1 serving Herbed Fish Amandine
1 serving Fabulous Pilaf
Steamed broccoli as desired
1 sliced orange with 2 tablespoons "Coconut" Sauce

27

What Happens When Your Weight Goes Up?

One of the most dreaded things that can happen to a dieter after reaching ideal weight is to begin to regain those unwanted pounds (kilos). If this does happen to you, ask yourself several questions. Have I been on my program of maintenance exactly as I should? Am I being realistic about my answer to the first question? Could there be something else besides excess caloric intake or decreased physical activity to explain my weight gain?

The first question is an obvious one. From the moment we are "cured" and reach our ideal weight we will find ourselves subject to temptation to overeat, either from our own inner desires, or from external sources like feeders. It is a common problem among dieters that we seem to build up a stack of I.O.U.'s to ourselves while we are dieting. After the dieting is over and the maintenance phase begins we may start to call in some of those I.O.U.'s and overeat "just a little bit." My standard answer to the claim of overeating "just a little bit" is to ask patients if they have heard of someone being "just a little bit pregnant."

Of course, there is no such thing! You are either completely pregnant or you are not. You are completely on your diet, or you are not, and the sooner a patient with a weight problem realizes this, the better off he or she is. This is where realistic evaluation of your situation comes into the picture. You are only fooling yourself if you try to cover up your mistakes by faulty reasoning and hiding the truth from yourself. When it comes down to it, each person has only his own self to satisfy. The doctor and family and friends may be involved peripherally, but the personal and inner communication of the patient to herself or himself is the most important. Be honest with yourself.

After ruling out dietary transgressions and a decreased energy output as the causes, we must consider some physiological causes for the weight gain. Most rapid weight gain is water, not fat. The scales have no pity, however, and weigh a pound of fat and a pound of water the same.

One of the most common causes of fluid retention is the intake of certain medications. Most of these medications have been prescribed by a physician for another problem that the patient has. I cannot fault the physician for using them and most are given for relatively short periods of time. If you are aware of the medicine's action in causing fluid retention, continue the medication as directed, but don't let the lack of weight loss or even weight gain upset you.

Almost every form of medication designed for anti-inflammatory action on arthritis, bursitis, or related conditions can cause fluid retention. A partial list includes Indocin, Butazolidin, cortisone-like steroids, Nalfon, Motrin and Tolectin. If your doctor prescribes them, use them for the short time he wishes you to and then marvel at the rapid weight loss once they are discontinued.

A second and most annoying cause is cyclic changes in the female hormone levels. Just prior to the menstrual flow there is a buildup of these female hormones in the bloodstream of many women, and this excessive amount of estrogens causes a marked bloating. The problem seems to be related to this excessive amount of estrogen, and the solution must be explained in an oversimplified manner with apologies to the scientists who might read this.

The explanation should be preceded by a statement that what I am proposing is not a true picture of the biochemistry, but a pragmatic lay explanation. There are three types of estrogen found in the human female that are of importance. I will call them estrogens I, II, and III. Estrogen I is the primary secretion of the ovaries and is the major female hormone put out during the part of the menstrual cycle just preceding the bleeding phase. It is converted, primarily by the liver, into estrogen II, and finally into estrogen III. If the liver is unable to process the large amounts of estrogen I, this hormone builds up in the body and causes the typical swelling, bloating and discomfort of the premenstrual distress syndrome.

Only estrogen III can be excreted, or gotten rid of, by the body in any great quantities. Once the estrogen is "used" by the body it must be excreted, but if it cannot be processed by the liver the symptoms continue. The machinery that does the conversion to the excretable form is present in the liver enzymes and these enzymes must have certain elements of the B-complex to work, particularly vitamin B-6.

Therefore, in order to utilize, process and excrete the estrogen produced by the female at this time in her cycle, we must have adequate B-complex and particularly B-6. I have found through experience that heavy doses of B-6, sometimes as high as 100 milligrams four times daily are required over several days to get a result. This is an unproven, untested and possibly unscientific solution to the problem, *but it works!* I am aware that many physicians use diuretics, but I have found far less side effects from B-complex and B-6 than I have ever found when I used diuretics for the same symptoms. In fact, I have treated hundreds of women with B-6 for this problem and have *never* had a problem. I leave it to you to decide what you and your doctor will use if this problem exists for you.

Another cause of fluid retention is stress. Anything that is out of the ordinary could be classified as stress. Personal illness, pregnancy, severe emotional strain, surgery and illness in family members can all cause the body to react to this outside or internal stress with what is known as the stress response. One of the stress responses is the secretion of certain hormones from the adrenal glands that help deal with the stress, but also have a salt-retaining action.

Whatever the cause of the fluid retention, it should be temporary. With proper management the fluid will eventually be released and the weight will return to the desired level. The important thing is to know what is going on and not to get discouraged enough to go on a binge with a "What the Hell, if I'm going to gain even though I am good, why not enjoy myself?" You would be surprised to know how many patients have fallen into this trap over the years.

There are possibly other causes of weight and/or fluid retention, but these three groups of causes or etiologies are the most commonly seen. Again, please don't fall prey to the trap of taking diuretics for the *sole* purpose of "losing weight." This is an unhealthy and potentially dangerous practice. That is *not* to say that if your doctor is prescribing this type of medication for hypertension, heart disease, or related problems, you should not take them. Your doctor knows you best of all and should be obeyed when it comes to treatment methods.

THE ONE-WEEK PANIC DIET (THE FABULOUS FRUCTOSE EMERGENCY DIET)

The diet that follows is only to be followed for one week at a time. You should return to your usual maintenance program beginning on the eighth day. It is to be used when weddings, parties, birthdays, funerals or other stress and eating occasions strike down your will to follow your maintenance routine. It is to be consumed exactly as given, but without the usual sprinkling of the condiment known as guilt. You don't have to feel guilty as this is a feeling that feeds on itself and grows. Take the attitude that you are human and you made an expected mistake.

This doesn't mean that you ignore the behavior and that you don't try to prevent recurrences. Learn from your mistakes and your problems and try to make the interval between such

31

problem eating episodes a little greater each time. Now for the one-week panic diet.

FABULOUS FRUCTOSE EMERGENCY DIET (800 CALORIES)

2 quarts of water throughout the day
2-gram (8-calorie) fructose tablets as needed (not to exceed 8)

BREAKFAST
1 fruit portion
1 low- or medium-fat protein portion
1 starch portion
1 nonfat milk portion

LUNCH
3 low-fat protein portions
1 starch portion
1 vegetable portion
1 fruit portion
Free foods as desired

DINNER
3 low-fat protein portions
1 vegetable portion
1 fruit portion
Free foods as desired

SAMPLE FABULOUS FRUCTOSE EMERGENCY DIET MENU

BREAKFAST
½ grapefruit
1 soft-boiled egg, or ¼ cup liquid egg substitute

1 slice of whole-wheat toast
1 cup nonfat milk

LUNCH
3 ounces of chicken without skin
1 slice of Canyon Ranch Bread
1 tomato, sliced
¾ cup fresh strawberries with 1 teaspoon fructose

DINNER
Tossed green salad with 2 tablespoons Fabulous Dressing
4½ ounces fresh fish cooked without added fat
½ cup steamed carrots
½ cup sliced peaches with 2 tablespoons "Amaretto" Sauce

Questions and Answers

QUESTION: What about lecithin in my diet? I have been using a large amount of this substance in my diet and want to keep it up. Will it slow down my weight loss?

ANSWER: Yes! If you figure that lecithin has about two-thirds the calories of an equal weight of fat you will be approximately correct. The only difference between lecithin and body fat (triglyceride) is that lecithin has only two fatty-acid chains attached to a glycerol molecule and fat has three. These two fatty-acid chains have a tremendous amount of concentrated energy as usable calories and these calories must be accounted for. I personally use choline and methionine for the same purpose and expect I get the same results (some people dispute the effectiveness of any of these) as I would by taking lecithin, with negligible calories as a bonus.

QUESTION: I have trouble finding fructose in my stores locally. How can I get a supply so I can use it for my diet?

ANSWER: Fortunately there are now three acceptable forms of fructose. The two-gram chewable tablets and the three-gram granule packets have been available in most stores, but now there is a syrup with 90 percent fructose that can be used for cooking and for adding to beverages. The first two forms are in relatively short supply, but the syrup is available in tankcar lots and no shortage of it is anticipated.

QUESTION: How much fructose is in the syrup, and didn't you warn us about using bulk fructose?

ANSWER: There are 6 grams in each level teaspoon of fructose-90 syrup. It is true that the granules should not be purchased in bulk (except for cooking) because of the tendency to get too much per spoonful. A "level" teaspoon of granules to some dieters can resemble the Matterhorn, with what winds up being over two teaspoons piled onto a teaspoon measurer. Fortunately, the syrup doesn't pile up like that and is all right to use with a measuring spoon or container.

QUESTION: You mention that the syrup is 90 percent fructose. What about the rest of the contents?

ANSWER: The remainder of the contents are 1 percent complex carbohydrates and 9 percent glucose. Since you are getting no more than about 15 to 20 grams of fructose as the syrup it means that 9 percent, or no more than 2 grams of glucose, should be consumed each day, a negligible amount with little or no effect on the glucose-insulin trap.

QUESTION: What is the Ski Slope Syndrome and how could it affect my diet?

ANSWER: This is the phenomenon mentioned earlier under another name. It derives its name from the tendency of a dieter who goes off his diet to say, "What the Hell. I've blown it anyhow, why not go ahead and really go on an eating binge?" It is almost like a beginner at skiing who gets to the top of a long slope and pushes off. After a few feet the momentum picks up so much that the inexperienced person cannot stop until the bottom of the slope (or the top of the weight curve) is reached. This is a nightmare for both doctor and patient and can only be stopped by prior education and instructions as to what to do when the dreaded day comes that a dieting mistake is made.

QUESTION: What is a Diet Bullet?

ANSWER: This is a preparation of protein powder, fruit, fructose and nonfat milk that shoots down the dieter's hunger in its tracks. It is tasty and can be prepared with a minimum of effort and expense for use as a meal in itself, as a snack, or as a preventive pre-party snack when you are afraid that you might overdo things. The fruits can be pre-measured and frozen in

35

packets ahead of time. The nonfat milk is readily available and the Diet Bullet packets are soon to be available in pre-measured packets for convenience by at least two companies. My problem after taking a Diet Bullet in the morning is remembering that I need to eat lunch. The fructose and protein combination aborts hunger so well that an alarm clock is called for to remind a patient when the next meal should be eaten.

PART TWO

COOKING

Introduction

Fructose is indeed *fabulous!* Not only does it help to keep away those terrible hunger pangs associated with reducing diets; it also helps to heighten and sharpen flavors in the absence of salt. Therefore it is a great help to people on sodium-restricted diets.

When I was working on *The Secrets of Salt-Free Cooking,* a low-sodium cookbook, I discovered that one of the most important "secrets" for successfully seasoning without salt is a combination of fructose and lemon juice. Along with small amounts of fructose and lemon juice, all other herbs and spices can be used as desired for additional flavor. You will find that all foods, even vegetables, taste better prepared in this manner.

We are all so used to having our foods "hyped" with salt, the great dietary whitewash, that we forget how truly delicious the natural flavors of many usually oversalted foods can be. Even a soft-boiled egg is better with a pinch of fructose and a little lemon juice than it is with salt.

Although fructose is usually far sweeter than sucrose (ordinary table sugar), in fact about one and one-half times as sweet, there are instances when it is *not* appreciably sweeter. Fructose is not as sweet when it is in something hot as it is when it is in something cold. For this reason you will find I use more of it in recipes where the sweetness level should be high and the dish is going to be served hot than I do in recipes for something to be served cold. Also, the pH balance (a value used

39

to express relative acidity and alkalinity) of the other ingredients combined with fructose makes a difference in the level of sweetness and the sharpness of the flavor.

For these reasons it is not possible simply to replace the sugar called for in a recipe with a lesser amount of fructose and always achieve the desired result. All of the recipes in this book have been developed to utilize and maximize the very best qualities of fructose. The recipes call for granular fructose except where liquid fructose is specified. Each recipe has been tested many times to assure you of success. Nothing is more frustrating than to buy a cookbook with untested recipes, buy all the ingredients necessary to make dinner, and then end up with a disappointing failure—AND no dinner.

For several years I have been replacing sucrose and all artificial sweetners with fructose. Because I write only in the low-calorie field, fructose first impressed me as a sweetener because I was able to reduce calories without using artificial substitutes. After working with fructose for several months I realized that not only was I able to reduce calories, I was also achieving much better flavor with fructose than with any other form of sweetener. When using liquid fructose I could also greatly reduce the amount of oil used in baking, thereby further reducing the calories. Another decided advantage in using fructose for baking is that the cooking time is shortened, and therefore valuable energy is saved.

My own work in recipe development with fructose has led me into many other fields in the food industry. I am a consultant for several food companies and I write product books for Diet Delight, a division of California Canners and Growers, for C. G. Whitlock Process Company, and for Batter-Lite Foods, Inc.

I think you will find that after going on the Fabulous Fructose Diet, feeling better and looking younger than you have in years, you will also love using the recipes in this book to become the most talked-about gourmet cook in town.

JEANNE JONES

Stocks and Soups

Making your own stocks takes so little time and makes a big difference in the flavor of your soups and sauces. It also is much less expensive to make your own stocks, particularly if you take the French housewife approach and keep a couple of plastic bags in the freezer for bones and meat, one for beef and veal, the other for poultry. Lamb, ham and pork bones are not good for making stock because their flavor is too strong.

I have purposely left salt out of the stock recipes, replacing it with fructose as a flavor heightener, so that they will also be useful to people on sodium-restricted diets.

Because I like soups served both hot and cold, I have included recipes in this section which will be equally good served either way. In fact it is a great time saver always to make twice as much soup as you plan to serve and freeze the remaining portion to be served on another occasion. I have also given a great variety of uses with my soup recipes; some may be served as a very light first course while others can be served as the main dish for the entire meal.

Beef Stock

4 pounds beef or veal bones
3 large onions, cut into
quarters
2 carrots, scraped and sliced
6 garlic cloves
4 parsley sprigs
2 whole cloves
1 teaspoon celery seeds
1 teaspoon fructose

1 teaspoon dried thyme
1 teaspoon dried marjoram
2 bay leaves
¼ teaspoon peppercorns
1½ cups tomato juice (one 12-ounce can)
Defatted beef drippings (optional)
Distilled water

1. Preheat the oven to 400°. Brown the bones in a roasting pan for 30 minutes.
2. Add the onions, carrots and garlic and brown together for another 30 minutes, or until ingredients are a rich, deep brown in color.
3. Put the browned meat and vegetables in a large pot or soup kettle with the remaining ingredients.
4. Add cold distilled water to cover by 1 inch. Bring to a boil, then reduce heat and simmer slowly for 5 minutes; remove any scum that forms on the top.
5. Cover, leaving the lid ajar about 1 inch to allow steam to escape, and simmer slowly for at least 5 hours; ten hours are even better if you will be around to turn off the heat.
6. When the stock has finished cooking, allow it to come to room temperature. Refrigerate the stock, uncovered, overnight.
7. When the fat has hardened on the surface of the stock, remove it. Warm the defatted stock until it becomes liquid.
8. Strain the liquid and taste. If the flavor of the stock is too weak, boil it down to evaporate more of the liquid and concentrate its strength.
9. Store the stock in the freezer in the size container you will be using most frequently. You can then take the stock directly from the freezer and melt it whenever you need it.

Makes about 2½ quarts (10 cups) stock.

1 cup contains approximately:
    Calories negligible when defatted
    0 mg. cholesterol when defatted
    83 mg. sodium

Turkey Stock

1 turkey carcass	1 teaspoon dried thyme
3 onions, cut into quarters	1 teaspoon dried marjoram
2 carrots, scraped and sliced	¼ teaspoon peppercorns
5 garlic cloves	Defatted turkey drippings (op-
2 bay leaves	tional)
2 teaspoons dried basil	Distilled water
1 teaspoon fructose	

1. Break up the turkey carcass and put it in a large pot or soup kettle.
2. Add all other ingredients and add cold distilled water to cover by 1 inch.
3. Cover, leaving the lid ajar about 1 inch to allow the steam to escape. Simmer slowly for 4 to 8 hours, depending upon how much time you have to watch the stock.
4. Cool to room temperature and proceed exactly as you do for Beef Stock, preceding.

Makes 1½ to 2 quarts (6 to 8 cups) stock.

1 cup contains approximately:
    Calories negligible when defatted
    0 mg. cholesterol when defatted
    36 mg. sodium

43

Chicken Stock

3 pounds chicken parts
(wings, backs, necks)
1 whole stewing chicken (optional)
2 carrots, scraped and cut into
pieces
3 onions, cut into quarters

5 garlic cloves
2 parsley sprigs
2 bay leaves
1 teaspoon dried basil
1 teaspoon fructose
¼ teaspoon peppercorns
Distilled water

1. Put the chicken parts (and the whole chicken if you want to cook one in addition to making stock) and all other ingredients in a large pot or soup kettle.
2. Add cold distilled water to cover by 1 inch. Slowly bring to a boil.
3. Cover, leaving lid ajar about 1 inch to allow steam to escape. Simmer very slowly for 3 hours, until the whole chicken is tender.
4. Remove whole chicken and continue to simmer stock with chicken parts for 3 to 4 hours.
5. Cool stock to room temperature and put in the refrigerator, uncovered, overnight.
6. When the fat has hardened on the surface of the stock, re-move it. Warm the defatted stock until it becomes liquid.
7. Strain the liquid and taste. If the flavor of the stock is too weak, boil it down to evaporate more of the liquid and concentrate its strength.
8. Store the stock in the freezer in the size container you will use most often. You can then take the stock directly from the freezer and melt it whenever you need it.

   Cooking a stewing chicken while making stock is helpful in two ways: first it adds flavor to the stock; and secondly, it gives you a beautifully seasoned chicken for your dinner or

44

many other dishes such as soups, salads, sandwiches and a variety of both hot and cold entrées.

Makes 2½ quarts (about 10 cups) stock.

1 cup contains approximately:
Calories negligible when defatted
0 mg. cholesterol when defatted
106 mg. sodium

Fish Stock

2 pounds fish heads, bones and trimmings	1 carrot, scraped and sliced
2½ quarts distilled water	1 teaspoon dried marjoram
3 onions, sliced	1 teaspoon fructose
6 parsley sprigs	¼ teaspoon peppercorns
	¼ cup fresh lemon juice

1. Bring all ingredients to a boil and simmer, uncovered, for 45 minutes.
2. Line a colander or strainer with damp cheesecloth and strain the fish stock through it.
3. Cool to room temperature and store in the refrigerator. If you are not planning to use the fish stock within 2 days, store it in the freezer.

Makes 2 quarts (8 cups) stock.

1 cup contains approximately:
Calories negligible
0 mg. cholesterol
35 mg. sodium

Beef Consommé

(Clarified Beef Stock)

2 egg whites
4 cups Beef Stock (see index)
2 teaspoons dried chervil
2 parsley sprigs
1 teaspoon fructose

1 cup chopped green onion
tops
Freshly ground black pepper to
taste

1. Beat the egg whites with a wire whisk until they are slightly frothy. (If you are going to serve consommé hot or cold, you will want it beautifully clear; the addition of egg whites clarifies it.)
2. Add 1 cup of the cold stock to the egg whites and beat lightly together.
3. Put the other 3 cups of stock in a very clean saucepan with all remaining ingredients. (It is not necessary to add the other ingredients, but the consommé will have a much better flavor if you do.)
4. Bring the stock to a boil and remove from the heat.
5. Slowly pour the egg white and stock mixture into the balance of the stock, stirring with a wire whisk as you do.
6. Put the saucepan back on very low heat and mix gently until it starts to simmer.
7. Put the pan half on the heat and half off so that it is barely simmering; turn the pan around every few minutes. Simmer for 40 minutes.
8. Line a colander or a strainer with 2 or 3 layers of damp cheesecloth.
9. Allow stock to drain, undisturbed, until it has all seeped through. Then store until ready to use.

Makes 1 quart (4 cups) consommé.

Each cup contains approximately:
    Calories negligible
    0 mg. cholesterol
    10 mg. sodium

Court Bouillon

1½ quarts distilled water	2 bay leaves
2 cups dry white wine	1 teaspoon fructose
1 lemon, unpeeled and sliced	½ teaspoon celery seeds
1 carrot, scraped and sliced	¼ teaspoon peppercorns
1 onion, sliced	2 tablespoons fresh lemon
2 garlic cloves, cut into halves	juice

1. Combine all ingredients and simmer, covered, for 45 minutes.

    This court bouillon may be made ahead of time and used many times. When planning to reuse it, strain before storing; after each use store in the freezer.

    Any time you are going to cook shrimp, crab or lobster, or poach any fish, prepare the court bouillon first. Of course you can use fish stock for poaching fish, but this court bouillon is much faster and easier to make and completely satisfactory. You just cannot compare seafood cooked in plain water to seafood cooked in court bouillon. Always be careful not to overcook seafood because overcooking makes it tough. For example, when cooking shrimps never allow them to simmer for more than 2 minutes; then cool them in the court bouillon.

Makes 2 quarts (8 cups) bouillon.

1 cup contains approximately:
    Calories and sodium negligible because it is used only as a
    poaching liquid
    0 mg. cholesterol

Cold Consommé with Mushrooms

¼ cup fresh lemon juice
1 cup thinly sliced fresh mushrooms
2 cups Beef Consommé (see index), cold
4 tablespoons low-fat yogurt
5 teaspoons caviar

1. Pour lemon juice over thinly sliced mushrooms and put them in the refrigerator for at least 2 hours.
2. Add the sliced mushrooms and lemon juice to the 2 cups of cold consommé and mix well.
3. Put the consommé in 4 chilled bowls or icers. Put 1 tablespoon of yogurt on top of each one. Put 1¼ teaspoons of caviar on top of each spoonful of yogurt.

Makes 4 servings.

Each serving contains approximately:
 ¼ low-fat protein portion
 27 calories
 21 mg. cholesterol
 160 mg. sodium

Egg Flower Soup

3 cups Chicken Stock (see index)
2 eggs
2 tablespoons chopped chives or green onion tops

1. Bring the chicken stock to a boil.
2. Beat the eggs until they are frothy.
3. Slowly pour the beaten eggs into the boiling chicken stock, stirring constantly with a fork.
4. Continue to stir the soup rapidly until the eggs are shredded and look like long strings.
5. Serve very hot. Sprinkle the top of each bowl of soup with chopped green onion tops and put soy sauce on the table. A few drops in the soup are delicious (if you're on a sodium restricted diet, forget this).

Makes 4 servings.

Each serving contains approximately:
½ medium-fat protein portion
38 calories
126 mg. cholesterol
30 mg. sodium

Egg Sprout Soup

(Low-cholesterol egg flower soup)

3 cups Chicken Stock (see index)
2 egg whites
1 cup bean sprouts
1 tablespoon soy sauce
2 tablespoons finely chopped chives or green onion tops

1. Bring the chicken stock to a boil.
2. Beat the egg whites with a fork until slightly frothy.
3. Steam the bean sprouts until crisp-tender, for 2 to 3 minutes.

Recipe continues . . .

4. Slowly pour the beaten egg whites into the boiling chicken stock, stirring constantly with a wire whisk.
5. Add the bean sprouts and soy sauce.
6. Serve very hot. Sprinkle the top of each bowl with the chopped chives or green onion tops.

Makes 4 servings.

Each serving contains approximately:
Free food, calories negligible
0 cholesterol
284 mg. sodium

Stracciatella alla Romana

4 cups Chicken Stock (see index)
2 eggs
⅛ teaspoon ground nutmeg
¼ teaspoon fructose

1 tablespoon grated Romano cheese
2 tablespoons minced fresh parsley

1. Bring the chicken stock to a boil.
2. Combine the eggs, nutmeg, fructose and Romano cheese and beat thoroughly.
3. Add the parsley to the beaten egg mixture and pour the entire mixture into the boiling stock, stirring continuously until the eggs are cooked. This only takes a minute.
4. Ladle the soup at once into 6 bowls.
    I have always considered Stracciatella alla Romana to be the Italian version of Chinese egg flower soup, and I like it even

50

better. It is a very subtle and light first course to a normally heavier Italian entrée.

Makes 6 servings.

Each serving contains approximately:
    ½ medium-fat protein portion
    38 calories
    85 mg. cholesterol
    46 mg. sodium

Calcutta Consommé

3 cups Chicken Stock (see
    index)
3 cups tomato juice
1 tablespoon fresh lemon juice
1 teaspoon fructose

⅛ teaspoon salt
⅛ teaspoon curry powder
2 whole cloves
8 thin lemon slices for garnish

1. Combine all ingredients except the lemon slices in a saucepan and bring to a boil.
2. Reduce heat and simmer for 10 minutes.
3. To serve, place a thin slice of lemon on top of each bowl of consommé.

Makes 8 servings.

Each serving contains approximately:
    1 vegetable portion
    25 calories
    0 mg. cholesterol
    217 mg. sodium

51

Gazpacho

(Cold Mexican Soup)

4 cups tomato juice
1 small onion, chopped
1 small cucumber, peeled and
   chopped
1 small green bell pepper,
   seeded and chopped
2 canned green chiles, seeded
   and chopped
1 garlic clove, chopped
2 teaspoons Worcestershire
   sauce

1 teaspoon fructose
½ teaspoon seasoned salt
¼ teaspoon ground cuminseed
¼ teaspoon freshly ground
   black pepper
1 drop of Tabasco (optional)
1 large tomato, finely diced
2 tablespoons finely chopped
   chives or green onion tops
2 lemons, quartered lengthwise

1. Put 2 cups of the tomato juice and all other ingredients except the diced tomato, chopped chives and lemon wedges in a blender container and blend until smooth.
2. Slowly add the remaining 2 cups of tomato juice to the blender container. Pour the mixture into a large bowl and add the chopped tomato.
3. Serve in chilled bowls or icers. Sprinkle the chopped chives evenly over each serving and garnish with a lemon wedge on the side.

Gazpacho is a delicious and low-calorie first course for luncheon or dinner.

Makes 8 servings.

Each serving contains approximately:
   1 vegetable portion
   25 calories
   0 mg. cholesterol
   392 mg. sodium

52

Beet Borscht

3 cups cooked beets
1 teaspoon garlic salt
⅛ teaspoon freshly ground
   black pepper
½ teaspoon ground allspice

1 teaspoon fructose
2½ cups buttermilk
2 tablespoons sour cream
6 lemon wedges

1. Combine all ingredients except sour cream and lemon wedges in a blender container and blend until smooth.
2. Pour the contents of the blender into a saucepan and heat to desired temperature. *Do not boil!*
3. Pour the borscht into 6 soup bowls and put 1 teaspoon of sour cream on top of each serving. Garnish each serving with a lemon wedge.

   This soup is also good served cold. If you are serving it cold, do not heat. Instead, refrigerate until cold and serve in chilled bowls or icers.

Makes 6 servings.

Each serving contains approximately:
   1 vegetable portion
   ½ low-fat protein portion
   70 calories
   5 mg. cholesterol
   525 mg. sodium

Fresh Tomato Soup

4 cups diced peeled tomatoes
(6 medium tomatoes)
1 tablespoon corn oil margarine
1 medium onion, chopped

3 cups nonfat milk
½ teaspoon salt
1 teaspoon fructose
¼ teaspoon freshly ground
black pepper

1. Dip each tomato into boiling water to cover for about 10 seconds before peeling. This makes it much easier to peel them.
2. Dice the peeled tomatoes and set aside.
3. Melt the margarine in a large saucepan and add the onion.
Cook until the onion is soft and clear.
4. Add the tomatoes to the saucepan and continue cooking, covered, over medium heat for 30 minutes.
5. Pour the tomato-onion mixture into a blender container and
blend until smooth. Pour the tomato-onion mixture back into the
large saucepan and add the milk and all other ingredients.
6. Put the saucepan back on medium heat and heat to desired
serving temperature. *Do not boil!*

Makes 6 one-cup servings.

Each serving contains approximately:
   ½ non-fat milk portion
   1 vegetable portion
   ½ fat portion
   88 calories
   1.5 mg. cholesterol
   247 mg. sodium

Split-Pea Soup

1 pound split peas
2 quarts water
1 ham bone without meat
1 large onion, chopped
2 carrots, diced
2 large celery stalks, without
  leaves, chopped

1 bay leaf
½ teaspoon salt
1 teaspoon fructose
3 cups Chicken Stock (see
  index)
Sherry (optional)

1. Put all ingredients except chicken stock and sherry in a large soup kettle or stockpot. Bring to a boil.
2. Reduce heat to very low, cover, and cook for 5 to 6 hours.
3. Cool to room temperature and refrigerate overnight.
4. When cold remove all visible fat from the top. Remove ham bone and bay leaf.
5. Put the skimmed soup in a blender container, a little at a time, and purée.
6. Pour puréed soup into a large pan and add the chicken stock.
7. Heat well before serving. A teaspoon of sherry may be added to each bowl.

Makes 11 cups.

½ cup contains approximately:
    1 starch portion
    70 calories
    1 mg. cholesterol
    67 mg. sodium

Vichyssoise Surprise

2 cups water
½ teaspoon fructose
1 large head of cauliflower,
   broken into pieces
1 medium onion, sliced
2 cups nonfat milk

¼ teaspoon salt
⅛ teaspoon white pepper
⅛ teaspoon ground nutmeg
½ cup finely chopped chives or
   green onion tops

1. Bring the water to a boil in a large pan with a lid.
2. Add the fructose, cauliflower and onion. Cover and cook over high heat for about 10 minutes, or until the cauliflower can be easily pierced with a fork.
3. Put the cauliflower, onion and all of the water from the pan in a blender container. Add all other ingredients and blend until smooth in texture.

   This soup is delicious served hot, but I like it even better served cold in icers with finely chopped chives or green onion tops sprinkled over the top of each serving. Whenever I serve it cold, my guests all think it is vichyssoise and very high in calories. When I tell them there are no potatoes or cream in the soup they are amazed; that is why I called it Vichyssoise Surprise.

Makes 8 servings (5 to 6 cups).

Each serving contains approximately:
   ½ vegetable portion
   ¼ nonfat milk portion
   42 calories
   .5 mg. cholesterol
   104 mg. sodium

Scandinavian Fruit Soup

2 apples, peeled and diced (1½ cups), or 1½ cups canned unsweetened applesauce
2 pears, peeled and diced (1½ cups), or 1½ cups canned pears packed in water
2 cups water
½ teaspoon fructose
1 lemon slice
1 cinnamon stick
¼ cup fresh orange juice
1 teaspoon fresh lemon juice
¼ cup port wine
Mint sprigs for garnish (optional)

1. Combine fruits, water, fructose, lemon slice and cinnamon stick in a saucepan.
2. Cover and bring to a boil over medium heat. Continue to simmer for 20 minutes.
3. Remove from the heat and discard the lemon and cinnamon stick.
4. Pour the soup into a blender container and blend until smooth.
5. Add the orange and lemon juice and port and mix well.
6. Refrigerate until cold before serving.
7. Pour into 6 bowls. Garnish each serving with a mint sprig.

I like to serve this soup in icers as the first course of a brunch.

Makes 6 servings.

Each serving contains approximately:
1½ fruit portions
57 calories
0 mg. cholesterol
2 mg. sodium

57

Curried Orange Soup

2 cups fresh orange juice
2 tablespoons quick-cooking tapioca
1 teaspoon fructose

¼ teaspoon curry powder
⅛ teaspoon ground ginger
¼ cup plain nonfat yogurt

1. Combine all ingredients except the yogurt in a saucepan and allow to stand for 5 minutes.
2. Put the pan on medium heat and bring to a boil, stirring constantly.
3. As soon as soup comes to a boil, remove the pan from the heat and cool to room temperature.
4. Cover the pan and refrigerate until cold.
5. Before serving, add the yogurt and mix thoroughly.

Makes 4 servings.

Each serving contains approximately:
   1½ fruit portions
   65 calories
   1 mg. cholesterol
   9 mg. sodium

Chicken Soup

2 quarts Chicken Stock (see index), defatted and strained
4 teaspoons corn oil margarine
2 tablespoons all-purpose flour
¼ cup uncooked rice

1 celery stalk, finely chopped
3 cups sliced fresh mushrooms
1 teaspoon fructose
3 cups chopped cooked chicken
3 tablespoons Madeira wine

1. Put the chicken stock in a soup kettle and heat it to the boiling point.

2. While the stock is heating melt 2 teaspoons of the margarine in a pan and add 2 tablespoons flour.

3. Cook the flour and margarine for several minutes, stirring constantly. *Do not allow to brown!*

4. Slowy add about 2 cups of the hot stock to the flour mixture, stirring until it is completely blended.

5. Pour the stock-flour mixture back into the pot containing the rest of the stock and add the uncooked rice and celery. Simmer slowly for 30 minutes.

6. While the soup is simmering melt the additional 2 teaspoons of margarine in a pan and cook the mushrooms in it until they are tender.

7. Add the fructose, mushrooms and chopped chicken to the stock and simmer for 10 minutes longer. Just before serving, add the Madeira.

Makes 6 servings.

Each serving contains approximately:
  2 low-fat protein portions
  1 fat portion
  ½ starch portion
  190 calories
  45 mg cholesterol
  107 mg. sodium

Minestrone

1 cup dried kidney beans
2 tablespoons olive oil
3 garlic cloves, minced
½ pound lean pork, cut into ½-inch cubes
1 onion, finely chopped
2 medium zucchini squash, thinly sliced
1 leek, white part only, finely chopped
¼ teaspoon freshly ground black pepper
1 teaspoon dried orégano
1 teaspoon fructose
1 teaspoon dried sweet basil

2½ quarts Beef Stock (see index)
1 small head of cabbage
6 large romaine lettuce leaves, cut into strips
½ cup finely chopped fresh parsley
1 cup dry red wine
2 cups (one 16-ounce can) canned tomatoes, plus all the juice from the can
½ cup uncooked elbow macaroni
Fresh lemon juice
⅓ cup grated Parmesan cheese

1. Soak the kidney beans in cold water overnight.
2. In a skillet, heat the 2 tablespoons of olive oil.
3. Add the minced garlic and sauté until tender.
4. Add the cubed pork and sauté until well cooked and browned.
5. Add the onion, zucchini, leek, pepper, orégano, fructose and basil to the pork. Cover and cook for 10 minutes.
6. Bring the beef stock to a boil.
7. Drain the kidney beans and add them to the boiling stock.
8. Add the pork mixture from the skillet and mix well.
9. Add the cabbage, lettuce, parsley and wine and cook until the beans are tender, about 1½ hours.
10. Add the tomatoes and macaroni and cook for 15 minutes longer.
11. Before serving, add the lemon juice and mix thoroughly.

60

Sprinkle 1 scant teaspoon of the grated Parmesan cheese over the top of each serving.

Makes 16 servings.

Each serving contains approximately:
   ¼ medium-fat protein portion
   ¼ fat portion
   ½ vegetable portion
   1 starch portion
   113 calories
   15 mg. cholesterol
   41 mg. sodium

Strawberry Soup

3 cups sliced fresh or unsweetened frozen strawberries, chilled
1 cup unsweetened pineapple juice, chilled
2 teaspoons fructose
½ teaspoon vanilla extract

1. Put 2 cups of the sliced strawberries in a blender container. Set the remaining cup of strawberries aside to add later.
2. Add all other ingredients to the strawberries in the blender container and blend until smooth.
3. Pour the soup into 4 bowls. Add ¼ cup of the remaining strawberries to each bowl.

Makes 4 servings.

Each serving contains approximately:
   2 fruit portions
   76 calories
   0 mg. cholesterol
   2 mg. sodium

Sauces and Salad Dressings

Sauces and salad dressings are the most important recipes in a low-calorie cookbook. Steamed vegetables marinated in low-calorie dressings make marvelous hors d'oeuvre and salads served cold. They are also delicious when heated and served as the vegetable on the dinner plate. Fish, meat and poultry cooked without any added fat can be turned into gourmet entrées simply with the addition of an unusual low-calorie sauce.

In this section, I have placed the emphasis on fabulous fakes, very low in calories and fat content; however, I have also included a few of the classics which are so good they are worth saving up your fat portions all day.

Defatted Drippings

If you love gravy but don't eat it because it contains so much fat, and therefore so many calories, your problems are over—defat your drippings!

All drippings are defatted in the same manner. After cooking your roast beef, leg of lamb, chicken, turkey or whatever, remove it from the roasting pan and pour the drippings into a bowl. Put the bowl in the refrigerator until the drippings are cold and all of the fat has solidified on the top. Remove the fat and you have defatted drippings.

Now, if you are in a hurry for them because you want to serve your roast beef *au jus* with defatted drippings instead of "fat *jus*," then put the drippings in the freezer instead of the refrigerator. Put the roast in a warm oven to keep it warm. After about 20 minutes you can remove the fat, heat the *jus,* and serve.

I always defat my drippings when I roast meat or poultry and store these drippings in the freezer. Defatted drippings add extra flavor to your stocks and are better than stocks for making the gravy recipes on the following pages.

Mornay Sauce

1½ cups Béchamel Sauce (see index)
½ cup liquid nonfat milk
½ cup grated Gruyère or Swiss cheese
⅛ teaspoon ground nutmeg
⅛ teaspoon white pepper
¼ teaspoon fructose

1. Heat the Béchamel Sauce and add the milk, cheese, nutmeg, pepper and fructose.
2. Stir over low heat until the cheese is completely melted.

Makes 2 cups.

1 cup contains approximately:
    1½ fat portions
    ½ starch portion
    1 whole milk portion
    1 high-fat protein portion
    368 calories
    39 mg. cholesterol
    398 mg. sodium

Béchamel Sauce

(Basic White Sauce)

2 cups liquid nonfat milk, boiling
1 tablespoon corn oil margarine
2½ tablespoons sifted all-purpose flour
⅛ teaspoon salt
¼ teaspoon fructose

1. Put the milk in a saucepan on low heat.
2. In another saucepan melt the margarine and add the flour, stirring constantly. Cook the flour and margarine for 3 minutes *Do not brown!*
3. Take the flour-margarine mixture off the heat and add the simmering milk all at once, stirring constantly with a wire whisk.
4. Put the sauce back on low heat and cook slowly for 20 minutes, stirring occasionally. If you wish a thicker sauce, cook it for a little longer time.
5. Add the salt and fructose. If there are lumps in the sauce (but there shouldn't be with this method), put it in a blender container and blend.

Makes 1½ cups.

¾ cup contains approximately:
    1½ fat portions
    ½ starch portion
    1 nonfat milk portion
    182 calories
    2.5 mg. cholesterol
    283 mg. sodium
1½ cups contain approximately:
    3 fat portions

1 starch portion
2 nonfat milk portions
365 calories
5 mg. cholesterol
565 mg. sodium

Fabulous Beef Gravy

1 cup defatted beef drippings, or 1 cup concentrated Beef Stock
  (see index)
1 tablespoon cornstarch or arrowroot
1 tablespoon dehydrated onion flakes
1 teaspoon fructose

1. Heat the defatted drippings in a saucepan.
2. As soon as drippings become liquid, put a little of the liquid
in a cup and add the cornstarch or arrowroot.
3. Pour the arrowroot mixture into the rest of the drippings.
4. Add the dehydrated onion flakes and fructose.
5. Simmer until gravy thickens slightly.

   Beef stock can be frozen in ice-cube trays and used for individual servings of this gravy. For 1 serving, use 2 beef stock
ice cubes, ¼ teaspoon cornstarch or arrowroot, 1 teaspoon
chopped onion (optional), and ¼ teaspoon fructose.

Makes 1 cup gravy.

¼ cup contains approximately:
   Free food, calories negligible
   0 mg. cholesterol
   21 mg. sodium

Fabulous Chicken Gravy

1 cup defatted chicken drippings, or 1 cup concentrated
Chicken Stock (see index)
1 tablespoon cornstarch or arrowroot
⅛ teaspoon garlic powder
¼ teaspoon fructose

1. Heat the defatted drippings in a saucepan.
2. As soon as drippings become liquid, put a little of the liquid
in a cup and add the cornstarch or arrowroot.
3. Pour the arrowroot mixture into the rest of the drippings.
4. Add the other ingredients and simmer until gravy thickens
slightly.
   Chicken stock can be frozen in ice-cube trays and used for
individual servings of this gravy. For 1 serving use 2 chicken
stock ice cubes, ¼ teaspoon cornstarch or arrowroot, and 1 teaspoon chopped onion (optional).

Makes 1 cup gravy.

¼ cup contains approximately:
   Free food, calories negligible
   0 mg. cholesterol
   27 mg. sodium

Fabulous Turkey Gravy

2 cups defatted turkey drip-
    pings
2 tablespoons cornstarch or ar-
    rowroot
½ cup minced green onion
    tops

½ cup chopped fresh
    mushrooms
2 tablespoons minced parsley
¼ teaspoon fructose

1. Heat the defatted drippings in a saucepan.
2. As soon as drippings become liquid, put a little of the liquid
in a cup and add the cornstarch or arrowroot.
3. Pour the arrowroot mixture into the rest of the drippings.
4. Add all of the other ingredients and simmer until gravy
thickens slightly.

Makes 2 cups gravy.

¼ cup contains approximately:
      Free food, calories negligible
      0 mg. cholesterol
      15 mg. sodium

Cheese Sauce

1½ cups Béchamel Sauce (see index)
⅛ teaspoon white pepper
¼ teaspoon dry mustard
½ teaspoon fructose
½ cup grated sharp Cheddar cheese

1. Heat the Béchamel Sauce and add the pepper, dry mustard, fructose and grated cheese.
2. Stir over low heat until the cheese is completely melted.

Makes 2 cups.

1 cup contains approximately:
    1½ fat portions
    ½ starch portion
    1 nonfat milk portion
    1 high-fat protein portion
    278 calories
    33 mg. cholesterol
    476 mg. sodium

Fabulous Mustard Sauce

1½ tablespoons dry mustard
¼ cup cider vinegar
½ cup liquid egg substitute, or
    2 egg yolks

½ cup liquid nonfat milk
1 tablespoon corn oil margarine
3 tablespoons fructose

1. Combine the dry mustard with the vinegar and stir until the mustard is completely dissolved.
2. Combine the mustard-vinegar mixture with the liquid egg substitute and milk in a saucepan.
3. Slowly bring to a boil, stirring constantly with a wire whisk. Continue stirring for 30 seconds.
4. Remove from the heat and put the margarine on top of the sauce. *Do not stir!*
5. Allow to cool to room temperature.
6. Add the fructose and, again using a wire whisk, mix the sauce thoroughly.
7. Store in the refrigerator.

This is an excellent sauce for corned beef, hot dogs, baked ham; use your imagination!

Makes 1½ cups.

2 tablespoons contain approximately:
¼ fat portion
37 calories
.6 mg. cholesterol
36 mg. sodium

Garlic-Flavored Oil

1 cup corn oil
2 garlic cloves, peeled and quartered
¼ teaspoon fructose

Recipe continues . . .

1. Place the corn oil, garlic and fructose in a jar with a tight-fitting lid and allow to stand at room temperature for a full 24 hours.
2. Remove garlic from the oil.
3. Store in the refrigerator for various uses, such as making croutons for Caesar salad, garlic-flavored oil for salad dressing, sautéing onions, et cetera.

Makes 1 cup.

1 teaspoon contains approximately:
    1 fat portion
    45 calories
    0 mg. cholesterol
    trace sodium

Cuminseed Dressing

1½ cups Basic French Dressing (see opposite)
¼ teaspoon ground cuminseed

1. Add cuminseed to Basic French Dressing and mix thoroughly.
    The flavor of this dressing is better if allowed to stand for 24 hours before using. If you prefer a stronger cumin flavor, add a little more cuminseed to the dressing.

Makes 1½ cups dressing.

1 tablespoon contains approximately:
    2 fat portions
    90 calories
    0 mg. cholesterol
    139 mg. sodium

Basic French Dressing

1½ teaspoons salt
¼ cup red-wine vinegar
½ teaspoon fructose
¼ teaspoon freshly ground
  black pepper
1½ teaspoons fresh lemon
  juice

¾ teaspoon Worcestershire
  sauce
¼ teaspoon Dijon-style mustard
½ garlic clove, minced
¼ cup water
1 cup corn oil

1. Dissolve the salt in the vinegar.
2. Add all other ingredients except oil and mix well.
3. Slowly stir in the oil.
4. Pour into a jar with a tight-fitting lid and shake vigorously for 1 full minute. Store in the refrigerator.

This dressing makes an excellent marinade for cold cooked vegetables, a good marinade for meat before roasting or charcoal-broiling, as well as being my own favorite salad dressing. I use it as a base for other types of salad dressings.

Makes 1½ cups.

1 tablespoon contains approximately:
    2 fat portions
    90 calories
    0 mg. cholesterol
    139 mg. sodium

Italian Dressing

1½ cups Basic French Dressing (preceding recipe)
1 teaspoon dried orégano
½ teaspoon dried sweet basil
½ teaspoon dried tarragon
¼ teaspoon fructose

1. Add all ingredients to Basic French Dressing and mix thoroughly.

This dressing makes an excellent marinade for cold cooked vegetables to be served as an antipasto, the first course of an Italian meal.

Makes 1½ cups dressing.

1 tablespoon contains approximately:
2 fat portions
90 calories
0 mg. cholesterol
139 mg. sodium

Tarragon Dressing

1½ cups Basic French Dressing (see index)
1½ teaspoons dried tarragon

1. Using a mortar and pestle, crush the tarragon completely.
2. Add to the Basic French Dressing and mix thoroughly.

Makes 1½ cups dressing.

1 tablespoon contains approximately:
    2 fat portions
    90 calories
    0 mg. cholesterol
    139 mg. sodium

Vinaigrette Dressing

1½ cups Basic French Dressing (see index)
1 tablespoon capers, finely chopped
1 tablespoon finely chopped pimiento
1 tablespoon finely chopped chives
1 teaspoon finely chopped fresh parsley
1 hard-boiled egg white, finely chopped
¼ teaspoon paprika

1. Add all ingredients to Basic French Dressing and mix thoroughly.

Makes 1½ cups dressing.

1 tablespoon contains approximately:
    2 fat portions
    90 calories
    0 mg. cholesterol
    166 mg. sodium

Caesar Dressing

3 garlic cloves, peeled and
quartered
1 cup corn oil
1½ teaspoons salt
¼ cup red-wine vinegar
¼ teaspoon fructose
¼ cup water
¼ teaspoon freshly ground
black pepper
3 tablespoons freshly
squeezed lemon juice

1 teaspoon Worcestershire
sauce
¼ teaspoon Dijon-style mustard
½ garlic clove, minced
¼ cup grated Parmesan
cheese
3 anchovy fillets, finely
chopped

1. Twenty-four hours before making this dressing, add the quartered garlic cloves to the corn oil and put in a jar with a tight-fitting lid. Allow to stand at room temperature for a full 24 hours.
2. Remove the garlic from the oil and set the garlic-flavored oil aside.
3. Dissolve the salt in the vinegar.
4. Add all other ingredients except the garlic-flavored oil and mix well.
5. Slowly stir in the oil.
6. Pour into a jar with a tight-fitting lid and shake vigorously for 1 full minute.

   This Caesar Salad Dressing is the best I have ever had. When used to make Caesar Salad, even the world's most discriminating Caesar Salad buffs will not realize that an egg has not come close to the salad.

Makes 1½ cups dressing.

1 tablespoon contains approximately:
   2 fat portions
   90 calories
   .6 mg. cholesterol
   167 mg. sodium

Tartar Sauce

⅔ cup sour cream
2 tablespoons Mayonnaise (see index)
¼ teaspoon salt
½ teaspoon fructose
1 teaspoon lemon juice

2 teaspoons dill pickle juice
1 tablespoon minced onion
1 tablespoon chopped dill pickle
2 teaspoons capers

1. Put the sour cream, mayonnaise, salt, fructose, lemon juice and pickle juice in a blender container and blend until smooth.
2. Pour the mixture into a bowl and add onion, pickle and capers. Mix well and store in the refrigerator.

Makes 1 cup.

½ cup contains approximately:
   8 fat portions
   360 calories
   48 mg. cholesterol
   344 mg. sodium
1 tablespoon contains approximately:
   1 fat portion
   45 calories
   6 mg. cholesterol
   43 mg. sodium

75

Szechuan Dressing

¼ cup sesame seeds
⅔ cup corn oil
2 tablespoons lemon juice
2 tablespoons soy sauce (for
   sodium-restricted diets, 2
   tablespoons sherry)

2 tablespoons fructose
1 teaspoon garlic powder
1 tablespoon freshly grated
   gingerroot, or ½ teaspoon
   ground ginger
⅛ teaspoon cayenne pepper

1. Preheat the oven to 350°. Bake the sesame seeds on a cookie sheet in the center of the preheated oven for 8 to 10 minutes, or until they are golden brown. Watch them carefully as they burn easily. Set aside.
2. Combine all other ingredients and mix well. Add the toasted sesame seeds to the dressing and place in a jar with a tight-fitting lid. Shake vigorously for 1 full minute.
3. Place in the refrigerator for at least 24 hours before using.

   This is not only a delicious salad dressing, but also an excellent marinade for fish and chicken. It is also good over fruit, vegetables, fish, poultry and meat as a sauce. Sometimes I thicken it with a little pectin and use it as a dip for raw or cold cooked vegetables for hors d'oeuvre.

Makes 1 cup dressing.

1 tablespoon contains approximately:
   2½ fat portions
   113 calories
   0 mg. cholesterol
   2 mg. sodium with sherry
   130 mg. sodium with soy sauce

Mayonnaise

1 raw egg, at room tempera-
    ture
¼ teaspoon dry mustard
¼ teaspoon salt

¼ teaspoon fructose
1 tablespoon lemon juice
1 cup corn oil

1. Dip the egg into boiling water for 30 seconds.
2. Put the egg in a blender container with the dry mustard, salt, fructose, lemon juice and ¼ cup of the corn oil.
3. Turn on low speed. Immediately start pouring in the remaining corn oil in a steady stream.
4. Switch the blender to high speed for 3 or 4 seconds and then turn it off. Store mayonnaise in the refrigerator.

    If you do not have the time or inclination to make your own mayonnaise, I would recommend a fructose-sweetened commercial mayonnaise. (See Appendix 4 for suppliers of fructose products.)

Makes 1½ cups.

1 teaspoon contains approximately:
    1 fat portion
    45 calories
    5 mg. cholesterol
    13 mg. sodium

VARIATIONS: *Add ¼ garlic clove when serving with cold seafood. Substitute tarragon vinegar for the lemon juice as a sauce for vegetables. You can mix the tarragon vinegar mayonnaise with a little plain low-fat yogurt to make your fat portion go further.*

Curried Yogurt Dressing

1 cup plain low-fat yogurt
2 tablespoons Mayonnaise
(preceding recipe), or commercial fructose-sweetened
mayonnaise (see Appendix
4)

½ teaspoon curry powder
⅛ teaspoon ground ginger
¼ teaspoon salt
½ teaspoon fructose

1. Put all ingredients in a blender container and blend until smooth.

Makes 1 cup dressing.

½ cup contains approximately:
    3 fat portions
    ½ low-fat milk portion
    195 calories
    15 mg. cholesterol
    244 mg. sodium

Dilled Yogurt Dressing

1 cup plain low-fat yogurt
¼ cup red-wine vinegar
1 teaspoon salt
2 teaspoons fructose

2 teaspoons dillweed
⅛ teaspoon freshly ground
   black pepper

1. Combine all ingredients in a large mixing bowl and mix thoroughly.
    This dressing is even better the day after it is made.

Makes 1⅓ cups dressing.

2 tablespoons contain approximately:
    Food portions negligible
    22 calories
    3.6 mg. cholesterol
    257 mg. sodium

Green Goddess Dressing

1 cup plain low-fat yogurt
3 tablespoons Mayonnaise (see index) or commercial fructose-sweetened mayonnaise (see Appendix 4)
5 flat fillets of anchovies, drained and chopped
2 tablespoons tarragon vinegar

1 tablespoon red-wine vinegar
½ cup minced fresh parsley
¼ cup chopped green onion tops
⅛ teaspoon salt
¼ teaspoon fructose
Dash of white pepper

1. Put all ingredients in a blender container and blend until smooth and green.

Makes 2 cups dressing.

½ cup contains approximately:
    2 fat portions
    105 calories
    16 mg. cholesterol
    665 mg. sodium
1 tablespoon contains approximately:
    ¼ fat portion
    13 calories
    2 mg. cholesterol
    83 mg. sodium

Calorie-Cutter's Catsup

4 cups tomato juice
¼ cup wine vinegar
2 whole garlic cloves
¾ teaspoon fructose

1. Put tomato juice, vinegar and garlic in a saucepan and bring to a boil.
2. Reduce heat to very low and simmer for about 2½ hours, or until of desired thickness.
3. Remove from heat and cool to room temperature.
4. Remove garlic cloves and add fructose.
5. Store in a glass or plastic container in the refrigerator.

    Making your own catsup saves calories in this way: One-half cup of tomato juice is only 1 vegetable portion. Two tablespoons of commercial catsup is 1 fruit portion or 3 tablespoons is 1 starch portion. When you reduce 4 cups of tomato juice to 1½ cups as you do in this recipe, you get two tablespoons for only ¼ vegetable portion and 7 calories as opposed to 40 calories for commercial catsup.

Makes 1½ cups.

2 tablespoons contain approximately:
    ¼ vegetable portion
    7 calories
    0 mg. cholesterol
    81 mg. sodium

Skinny Dressing

1 teaspoon unflavored gelatin
1 tablespoon cool water
2 tablespoons boiling water
1 cup buttermilk
¼ cup sour cream

⅛ teaspoon salt
⅛ teaspoon dry mustard
1 tablespoon fructose
1½ teaspoons cider vinegar

1. Combine the unflavored gelatin and cool water and allow the gelatin to soften.
2. Add the boiling water to the softened gelatin and stir until the gelatin is completely dissolved.
3. Add the buttermilk to the gelatin and mix well.
4. Put the buttermilk-gelatin mixture in a blender container. Add all other ingredients and blend until smooth.
5. Store in a covered container in the refrigerator.

Makes 1½ cups dressing.

2 tablespoons contain approximately:
  18 calories
  3.3 mg. cholesterol
  48 mg. sodium

Mystery Dressing

¾ cup unsweetened pineapple
   juice
¾ cup tomato juice
1 tablespoon freshly squeezed
   lemon juice
½ teaspoon fructose
¼ teaspoon salt

1 garlic clove, pressed
⅛ teaspoon freshly ground
   black pepper
⅛ teaspoon dry mustard
1 tablespoon chopped pimiento
1 teaspoon capers, chopped

1. Combine pineapple juice, tomato juice, lemon juice, fructose and salt. Mix thoroughly until salt completely dissolves.
2. Add all other ingredients and mix thoroughly. Store in a tightly covered container in the refrigerator.
   This is a fine low-calorie dressing for all types of salad.

Makes 1½ cups.

1 tablespoon contains approximately:
   Free food, calories negligible
   0 mg. cholesterol
   38 mg. sodium

Fabulous Dressing

(A low-calorie, low-sodium, low-cholesterol fat-free taste treat.)

2 cups canned salt-free tomatoes, undrained
¼ cup freshly squeezed lemon
   juice
2 tablespoons red-wine vinegar
3 tablespoons finely chopped
   onion
2 garlic cloves, chopped

¼ teaspoon chili powder
¼ teaspoon dried orégano
¼ teaspoon ground cuminseed
¼ teaspoon freshly ground
   black pepper
¼ teaspoon fructose
⅛ teaspoon Tabasco

1. Put all ingredients into a blender container and blend until smooth.
2. Store in the refrigerator in a covered container.

Makes 2½ cups dressing.

2 tablespoons contain approximately:
   ¼ vegetable portion
   7 calories
   0 mg. cholesterol
   3.4 mg. sodium

Salads

The range of ingredients in salads is limitless. A salad can serve for a small, practically calorie-free side dish, or for a main course combining everything necessary for the main meal.

Salads can also be the most beautiful part of a meal. Always take a little extra time to garnish your salads with radish roses, carrot curls, or something.

Preparing your salad greens well ahead of time is extremely important. Wash them well and dry them thoroughly. Wrap them in damp towels and store in the refrigerator. Not only will your salad greens be more crisp but it will take far less salad dressing to coat each leaf completely. When you are counting calories and lowering fats, the less dressing the better.

You may wish to serve salad as a first course, a side dish, or after the entrée, or perhaps even as the entrée; regardless of how or when you plan to serve your salad, always serve it on very cold plates.

Christmas Relish

2 small oranges
2 tablespoons grated orange rind
⅔ cup fructose
1 pound (4 cups) fresh cranberries

1. Wash oranges well and grate 2 tablespoons of the rind. Be careful to grate only the orange-colored part.
2. Peel oranges and cut them into pieces; remove seeds and connecting membranes.
3. Place the orange pieces in a blender container with the grated rind and fructose. Mix well.
4. Add the cranberries, a few at a time, until all the berries have been blended into the relish. Don't blend too fine.
5. Place in a covered container in the refrigerator. Make the relish 3 or 4 days before you plan to use it if possible.

Makes 4 cups.

½ cup contains approximately:
    2 fruit portions
    80 calories
    0 mg. cholesterol
    1 mg. sodium

Soufflé-Textured Tuna Aspic

1 envelope unflavored gelatin
2 tablespoons cold water
1 tablespoon lemon juice
1 teaspoon fructose
¼ teaspoon salt
¾ cup Chicken Stock (see index), boiling
¾ cup cold water
2 cans (7 ounces each) water-packed tuna, drained

2 tablespoons capers
¼ cup finely chopped green pepper
¼ cup finely chopped celery
2 hard-boiled eggs, cut into round slices
1 can (2 ounces) pimiento, cut in strips

1. Combine the gelatin, cold water and lemon juice and allow to stand for 5 minutes for the gelatin to soften.
2. Add the fructose, salt, and boiling chicken stock and stir until the gelatin is completely dissolved.
3. Place the gelatin mixture in the refrigerator and chill until firm.
4. When firm, put the jelled stock into a blender container; add the cold water and blend until frothy.
5. Pour the mixture into a bowl and allow to stand until it starts to thicken.
6. Fold in all other ingredients except the sliced hard-boiled eggs and pimiento strips.
7. Place the egg slices and the pimiento strips in a design in the bottom of a 4-cup mold. I like to use a fish-shaped mold when making this aspic.
8. Pour the tuna aspic mixture over the top of the design and place in the refrigerator to jell until firm. This will take several hours or overnight.
9. Unmold carefully onto a bed of shredded lettuce and garnish with cold marinated vegetables. I like to serve Green Goddess Dressing (see index) over tuna aspic.

Makes 4 servings.

Each serving contains approximately:
2 low-fat protein portions
110 calories
126 mg. cholesterol
210 mg. sodium

VARIATION: *Soufflé-Textured Salmon Aspic: Use two 7-ounce cans of salmon, drained, instead of the tuna.*

Dilled Cucumbers

3 cucumbers, peeled and
   sliced paper-thin
½ teaspoon salt
¼ cup white-wine vinegar

¼ cup water
1½ teaspoons liquid fructose
2 teaspoons dillweed

1. Place the sliced cucumbers in a shallow bowl and sprinkle them with the salt.
2. Cover the cucumbers and put them in the refrigerator for 2 hours.
3. Pour off the water that has accumulated and add all the other ingredients, mixed together.
4. Put the cucumbers back in the refrigerator for 2 hours before serving.

Makes 3 cups.

1 recipe contains approximately:
1½ fruit portions
60 calories
0 mg. cholesterol
566 mg. sodium

Sauerkraut Salad

2 cups well-drained sauerkraut
½ cup grated carrots
1½ cups minced celery
1½ cups seeded and chopped
green bell pepper
½ cup seeded and chopped
sweet red pepper

½ cup finely chopped onion
⅓ cup white vinegar
¼ cup liquid fructose
1 teaspoon salt
Dash of freshly ground black
pepper

1. Put sauerkraut in a colander and rinse with cold water. Allow
to drain thoroughly.
2. Combine sauerkraut with all other ingredients.
3. Refrigerate all day or preferably overnight before serving.

Makes twelve ½-cup servings.

½ cup contains approximately:
    Free food, calories negligible
    0 mg. cholesterol
    495 mg. sodium

Colorful Coleslaw

1 head of cabbage, shredded (about 8 cups)
½ green bell pepper, seeded and thinly sliced
½ red bell pepper, seeded and thinly sliced
½ cup finely chopped chives or green onion tops
2 cups Skinny Dressing (see index)

1. Combine all ingredients and mix well before serving. (If red bell peppers are not available, use a whole green one, but of course the salad is more colorful with both kinds.)

Makes 12 servings.

Each serving contains approximately:
    1 vegetable portion
    ¼ fat portion
    28 calories
    4.4 mg. cholesterol
    71 mg. sodium

Curried Carrot Salad

3 cups grated peeled carrots
6 tablespoons raisins
½ cup Curried Yogurt Dressing (see index)

1. Mix all ingredients together well and serve on chilled plates.

Makes 6 servings.

Each serving contains approximately:
    1 vegetable portion
    ½ fruit portion
    ¼ fat portion
    57 calories
    2.5 mg. cholesterol
    42 mg. sodium

Party Pea Salad

3 cups fresh green peas, or 2 packages (10 ounces each) frozen
    peas
1 cup sour cream
1 cup finely chopped green onion tops
1 teaspoon seasoned salt
1 teaspoon fructose

1. Cook peas until almost done, then drain and cool.
2. Mix together sour cream, green onion tops and seasoned
salt.
3. Fold into the cooled green peas thoroughly.
4. Chill in the refrigerator for 2 days before serving.

**Makes 6 servings, or 12 servings if many other things are
served.**

Each serving contains approximately:
    1 vegetable portion
    2½ fat portions
    138 calories
    21 mg. cholesterol
    382 mg. sodium

South Seas Spoof

2 cups grated raw cauliflower
½ teaspoon coconut extract
½ teaspoon fructose
1 can (8 ounces) crushed pineapple packed in natural juice
Ground cinnamon for garnish

1. Combine the grated cauliflower, coconut extract and fructose and mix thoroughly.
2. Cover and refrigerate for at least 2 hours.
3. Combine the cauliflower mixture, crushed pineapple and all of the pineapple juice from the can and mix thoroughly.
4. Serve on cold plates and sprinkle the top of each serving with ground cinnamon.

Your guests will think they are eating shredded coconut, but coconut is a highly saturated fat so we "spoof."

Makes 4 servings.

Each serving contains approximately:
   ½ vegetable portion
   ¾ fruit portion
   52 calories
   0 mg. cholesterol
   6.5 mg. sodium

Wonderful Waldorf Salad

½ cup shelled walnuts
⅔ cup plain low-fat yogurt
2 tablespoons Mayonnaise (see index), or commercial fructose-sweetened mayonnaise (see Appendix 4)
1 teaspoon fresh lemon juice
1 teaspoon fructose

¼ teaspoon ground cinnamon
⅛ teaspoon curry powder
⅛ teaspoon salt
2 large red apples, diced
2 cups chopped celery
2 tablespoons finely chopped raisins
8 large lettuce leaves

Recipe continues . . .

1. Preheat the oven to 350°. Bake the walnuts in the oven for 8 to 10 minutes, or until golden brown. Watch them carefully as they burn easily. Set aside.
2. Combine all ingredients except the walnuts and lettuce leaves in a large mixing bowl and mix well.
3. Place the lettuce leaves on chilled plates and divide the salad evenly onto the 8 lettuce leaves.
4. Sprinkle toasted walnuts evenly over the top of each serving, 1 tablespoon per serving.

Makes 8 servings.

Each serving contains approximately:
    1½ fat portions
    1 fruit portion
    100 calories
    5.2 mg. cholesterol
    82 mg. sodium

Spinach Salad with Walnuts

¼ cup chopped walnuts
1½ pounds fresh spinach
½ cup Tarragon Dressing (see index)

1. Preheat the oven to 350°. Bake the walnuts on a cookie sheet in the oven for 8 to 10 minutes, or until golden brown. Watch them carefully as they burn easily. Set aside.
2. Wash the spinach and dry thoroughly.
3. Remove the stems from the spinach and tear leaves into bite-size pieces; there should be 6 cups.
4. Combine the spinach with ½ cup of Tarragon Dressing. Mix thoroughly and divide evenly among 8 chilled plates.

5. Sprinkle ½ tablespoon of the toasted walnuts over the top of each serving.

Makes 8 servings.

Each serving contains approximately:
　　1 vegetable portion
　　1½ fat portions
　　90 calories
　　0 mg. cholesterol
　　167 mg. sodium

Caesar Salad

1 head of romaine lettuce
1 cup bread croutons
1 tablespoon Garlic-Flavored Oil (see index)
1 tablespoon grated Parmesan cheese
½ cup Caesar Dressing (see index)

1. Several hours before serving, wash and dry the romaine lettuce thoroughly.
2. Tear it into bite-size pieces (there should be 6 cups) and put in a large bowl lined with a cloth to absorb any remaining moisture. Store in the refrigerator until ready to serve.
3. Put the croutons in a large jar with a tight-fitting lid. Add the Garlic-Flavored Oil and shake well.
4. Add the Parmesan cheese and shake again.
5. When ready to serve, remove the cloth from under the lettuce and add the salad dressing. Toss the salad until every leaf glistens. Add the croutons and again toss thoroughly.

Recipe continues . . .

Makes 6 servings.

Each serving contains approximately:
 ¼ starch portion
 3 fat portions
 152 calories
 0 mg. cholesterol
 268 mg. sodium

Apple and Cheese Salad

4 tablespoons sunflower seeds
1 large head of iceberg lettuce, finely chopped (6 cups)
4 small Delicious apples, diced (4 cups)
2 cups diced farmer cheese
½ cup Italian Dressing (see index)

1. Preheat the oven to 350°. Bake the sunflower seeds on a cookie sheet in the preheated oven for approximately 10 minutes, or until golden brown. Watch them carefully as they burn easily. Set aside.
2. Combine all other ingredients and toss well.
3. Serve on cold plates.
4. Sprinkle 1 tablespoon of the toasted sunflower seeds evenly over each serving.

Makes 4 servings, or at least 8 servings when served as a side dish.

Each serving contains approximately:
 4 fat portions
 1 fruit portion
 2 low-fat protein portions
 330 calories
 6 mg. cholesterol
 425 mg. sodium

94

Tabbouli

(Lebanese Salad)

1 cup uncooked bulgur
  (cracked wheat)
Hot water to cover bulgur
½ cup lemon juice
½ teaspoon salt
¼ teaspoon fructose
¼ teaspoon freshly ground
  pepper
1 garlic clove, minced

1 tablespoon water
3 tablespoons olive oil
2 tomatoes, diced
4 green onions, chopped
1 cup fresh minced parsley
½ cup fresh mint leaves,
  minced
24 small romaine lettuce
  leaves

1. Soak the bulgur in hot water for 30 minuues.
2. While the bulgur is soaking, make the dressing. Combine the lemon juice and salt and stir until the salt has dissolved.
3. Add the fructose, pepper, garlic and water and mix well.
4. Slowly add the oil.
5. Put the dressing in a jar with a tight-fitting lid and shake vigorously for 30 seconds. Set aside.
6. Drain the bulgur thoroughly.
7. Add the tomatoes, green onions, parsley and mint leaves to the bulgur.
8. Add the dressing and toss thoroughly. Chill well.
9. Serve on chilled salad plates with each serving surrounded by 4 romaine leaves; this salad is traditionally eaten by scooping it up on the leaves.

Makes 8 servings.

Each serving contains approximately:
  1 starch portion
  1 fat portion
  115 calories
  0 mg. cholesterol
  145 mg. sodium

Szechuan Shrimp Salad

1 small head of cauliflower, separated into bite-sized flowerets (about 3 cups)

½ pound fresh pea pods, or frozen pea pods when fresh are not available (about 2½ cups)

1 can (19 ounces) lotus root, drained and thinly sliced (about 2 cups)

½ cup Szechuan Dressing (see index)

1 pound shelled cooked shrimps (about 3 cups)

1. Place the cauliflower in a steamer and steam, covered, over rapidly boiling water for 3 minutes.

2. Remove the lid, add the pea pods to the cauliflower in the steamer, and continue to cook for 2 more minutes.

3. Remove the pea pods and the cauliflower from the heat and place under cold running water. Drain thoroughly and place in a large mixing bowl.

4. Add the sliced lotus root and the Szechuan Dressing and toss thoroughly.

5. Cover and refrigerate until thoroughly chilled.

6. To serve, add the shrimps and toss thoroughly.

   I like to serve this salad for luncheons and give my guests chopsticks to use instead of forks.

Makes 6 servings.

Each serving contains approximately
   1 vegetable portion
   2 low-fat protein portions
   2 fat portions
   203 calories
   96 mg. cholesterol
   208 mg. sodium

96

Hot Dog Salad

6 all-beef frankfurters
2 cups well-drained sauerkraut
½ cup grated carrot
1 cup finely chopped celery
1 cup finely chopped green bell pepper
1 cup finely chopped sweet red pepper
½ cup finely chopped onion

⅓ cup white vinegar
⅓ cup fructose
1 teaspoon salt
⅛ teaspoon freshly ground black pepper
1½ cups Fabulous Mustard Sauce (see index)
Fresh parsley for garnish
Sliced tomatoes for garnish

1. Slice each frankfurter lengthwise into halves and place under a broiler until lightly browned on both sides.
2. Remove from the broiler and cool to room temperature.
3. Chop the broiled frankfurters into small pieces and set aside.
4. Put the sauerkraut in a colander and rinse with cold water. Allow to drain thoroughly.
5. Combine the drained sauerkraut and all other ingredients and mix thoroughly.
6. Serve with Fabulous Mustard Sauce. Garnish with sprigs of fresh parsley and sliced tomatoes.

I like to serve toasted hot dog buns with this salad. It may also be made with leftover diced ham.

Makes 6 servings.

Each serving contains approximately:
    2 vegetable portions
    2 high-fat protein portions
    245 calories
    25.1 mg. cholesterol
    975 mg. sodium

Fabulous Curried Chicken Salad in Lettuce Bowls

20 walnut halves coarsely chopped (½ cup)
6 small heads of Boston lettuce
1 can (20 ounces) pineapple chunks packed in natural juice, drained
3 cups diced cooked chicken
½ cup Curried Yogurt Dressing (see index)

1. Bake the walnuts in a 350° oven for approximately 10 minutes, or until golden brown. Watch them carefully as they burn easily. Set aside.
2. Remove the hearts from the heads of Boston lettuce; be careful not to tear the outer leaves so that they can be used as "bowls" in which to serve the salad.
3. Tear 3 or 4 of the hearts into bite-sized pieces (approximately 8 cups of torn lettuce) to use for the salad.
4. Cut the drained pineapple chunks into halves and put them in a large mixing bowl.
5. Add the torn lettuce and chicken to the pineapple
6. Pour the dressing over the salad and toss thoroughly.
7. Place the lettuce "bowls" on large chilled plates. Divide the salad into the 6 lettuce "bowls."
8. Sprinkle the toasted walnuts evenly over the top of each serving. This makes a beautiful luncheon entrée.

Makes 6 servings.

Each serving contains approximately:
    1 fat portion
    1 vegetable portion
    1 fruit portion

98

2 low-fat protein portions
208 calories
47 mg. cholesterol
97 mg. sodium

Chef's Salad

½ head of cabbage, finely chopped
½ head of lettuce, finely chopped
1 large or 2 medium-sized tomatoes, diced
1 cup crumbled farmer cheese

1 cup diced Monterey Jack cheese
2 cups diced cooked turkey or chicken
¾ cup Basic French Dressing (see index)

1. Combine all ingredients and toss thoroughly with the dressing until the salad glistens.
2. Serve on chilled plates.

Makes 8 servings.

Each serving contains (with dressing) approximately:
    2 medium-fat protein portions
    2¼ fat portions
    246 calories
    43 mg. cholesterol
    477 mg. sodium

VARIATION: *Ham may be used in place of turkey or chicken, but the sodium figures will be higher.*

Vegetables and Grains

Vegetables are the dieter's best friends. They are colorful, delicious, and generally lower in calories than all other foods. Practically all vegetables can be eaten raw and many are even more delicious raw than cooked. The next time you are making a salad, try adding a little chopped raw broccoli, cauliflower or zucchini. Raw vegetables not only add taste but also texture to salads.

The best way to cook vegetables is to steam them. They are better for you nutritionally and, when steamed properly, they are more beautiful than vegetables cooked in any other manner. For this reason, I have started this section with vegetable steaming directions and a chart giving the time necessary to steam each vegetable until it is just crisp-tender.

Most of the recipes in this section call for steamed vegetables as ingredients; however, I have also included several recipes for vegetables prepared in other ways which I think are particularly outstanding.

Steaming Vegetables

When steaming vegetables, always make certain that the steamer basket is above the level of the water. The water should be boiling rapidly before the vegetables are covered and timing begins.

After steaming the vegetables for the correct length of time, immediately place them under cold running water. This stops the cooking quickly and preserves both the color and the texture of the vegetables. In fact your friends may accuse you of dyeing your green vegetables because they will be so bright and beautiful.

When reheating vegetables prepared in this manner, be careful not to overcook them in the reheating process or they will lose both their crispness and their color.

Whether you are going to be serving vegetables hot or cold, they can be prepared in advance and stored, covered, in the refrigerator. Many of the recipes in this section call for steamed vegetables; by being able to prepare them in advance, mealtime preparation time can be shortened greatly.

In the following vegetable steaming chart the time given for steaming each vegetable is for a crisp-tender preparation. I do not like soft, soggy vegetables. Mushy, colorless vegetables are not only tasteless, but have been robbed of much of their nutritional value by overcooking.

Fresh Vegetable Steaming Chart

	Minutes		Minutes
Asparagus	4	Eggplant	5
Beans:		Garlic	5
green	5	Jerusalem artichokes	8
lima	5	Jícama	10
string or snap	5	Kale	1 to 2
Bean sprouts	1 to 2	Kohlrabi, quartered	8 to 10
Beets, quartered	15	Leeks	5
Beet greens	3 to 5	Lettuce	1 to 2
Black radish, ½-inch		Lotus root, ¼-inch	
slices	5	slices	25
Breadfruit	10	Mint	1 to 2
Broccoli	5	Mushrooms	2
Brussels sprouts	5	Mustard greens	1 to 2
Cabbage, quartered	5	Okra	5
Carrots, ½-inch slices	5	Onions:	
Cauliflower:		green tops	3
flowerets	3	whole	5
whole	4 to 5	Palm hearts	5
Celery root	3 to 4	Parsley	1 to 2
Celery stalks	10	Pea pods	3
Chard	1 to 2	Peas	3 to 5
Chayote	3	Peppers, green and	
Chicory	1 to 2	red	2
Chiles	2 to 3	Poke	3
Chives	2 to 3	Potatoes:	
Cilantro	1 to 2	sweet, ½-inch slices	15
Collards	1 to 2	white, ½-inch slices	10
Corn:		Pumpkin	5
kernels	3	Radishes	5
on the cob	3	Rhubarb	5
Cucumber	2 to 3	Romaine lettuce	1 to 2
Dandelion greens	1 to 2	Rutabagas	8

	Minutes		Minutes
Shallots	2	summer	3
Spinach	1 to 2	zucchini	3
Squash:		Tomatoes	3
acorn	5	Turnips, quartered	8
Hubbard	5	Water chestnuts	8
spaghetti	5	Watercress	1 to 2

Marinated Vegetable Medley

3 cups assorted steamed vegetables, cold
1½ cups Basic French Dressing (see index)

1. Place the cold cooked vegetables in a nonmetal baking dish.
2. Pour the Basic French Dressing over the vegetables.
3. Cover and refrigerate for several hours or overnight before serving.

Follow the directions at the beginning of this section for steaming and cold-water rinsing to preserve color and texture. This recipe is designed to use up all of your leftover steamed vegetables from the previous few days in one delicious appetizer or salad course. The more variety you have in the vegetables used the more colorful your marinated medley will be.

Makes 6 servings.

Each serving contains approximately:
   1 vegetable portion
   2 fat portions
   115 calories
   0 mg. cholesterol
   556 mg. sodium, depending on assortment of vegetables used

103

Herbed Vegetable Medley

6 cups assorted steamed vegetables

3 tablespoons corn oil margarine

1 tablespoon fresh lemon juice

1 teaspoon fructose

1 teaspoon dried sweet basil, crushed

¼ cup finely chopped fresh parsley

¼ cup finely chopped chives or green onion tops

1. Steam the vegetables until just crisp-tender. Time will vary from one vegetable to another. (This recipe is also an excellent way to use the leftover steamed vegetables in the refrigerator.)
2. Melt the margarine in a large skillet.
3. Add all other ingredients except the vegetables and mix thoroughly.
4. Add the cooked vegetables and again mix thoroughly.
5. Heat just to serving temperature. Overheating will destroy both the color and the texture of the vegetables.

Makes 8 servings.

Each serving contains approximately:
    1 vegetable portion
    ¾ fat portion
    59 calories
    0 mg. cholesterol
    39 mg. sodium

Minted Carrots

1 pound carrots (8 small car-
    rots)
2 teaspoons arrowroot
½ cup water
2 tablespoons corn oil marga-
    rine

1 teaspoon fructose
½ teaspoon salt
½ cup finely chopped fresh
    mint leaves

1. Scrape the outside skin from the carrots and slice into ½-inch rounds.
2. Steam the carrots according to the steaming directions given at the beginning of this chapter.
3. Combine the arrowroot and water in a saucepan and stir until the arrowroot is thoroughly dissolved.
4. Cook, stirring constantly, until the mixture comes to a boil. Continue stirring until mixture is clear and thickened, about 2 minutes.
5. Remove from the heat. Add the fructose and salt and mix thoroughly.
6. Pour over the steamed carrots. Add the fresh mint and mix well. Minted carrots are particularly good with lamb.

Makes 8 servings.

Each serving contains approximately:
    1 vegetable portion
    ¾ fat portion
    48 calories
    0 mg. cholesterol
    161 mg. sodium

Zucchini in Herb "Butter"

3 cups sliced zucchini
2 tablespoons corn oil margarine
¼ teaspoon salt
½ teaspoon fructose

1 teaspoon dried sweet basil
¼ cup minced fresh parsley
¼ cup minced chives or green
   onion tops

1. Steam the zucchini according to steaming directions given at the beginning of this chapter.
2. Melt the margarine, add all other ingredients, and cook over low heat for 5 minutes.
3. Add the steamed zucchini to the herb butter sauce and mix thoroughly.

Makes 6 servings.

Each serving contains approximately:
   ½ vegetable portion
   1 fat portion
   58 calories
   0 mg. cholesterol
   69 mg. sodium

Creamed Spinach

2 pounds fresh spinach, chopped (7 cups)
1½ cups Béchamel Sauce (see index)
¼ cup grated Parmesan cheese
¼ teaspoon fructose
¼ teaspoon ground nutmeg

1. Steam the chopped spinach according to the steaming directions given at the beginning of this chapter.
2. Add all other ingredients and heat well together before serving.

Makes 6 servings.

Each serving contains approximately:
  ½ fat portion
  ½ low-fat meat portion
  ¾ starch portion
  1 vegetable portion
  106 calories
  3.3 mg. cholesterol
  171 mg. sodium

German Red Cabbage

1 small head of red cabbage, or ½ large head
2 teaspoons arrowroot
½ cup water

½ cup cider vinegar
2 tablespoons fructose
⅛ teaspoon salt
½ teaspoon caraway seeds

1. Shred cabbage and steam according to the steaming directions given at the beginning of this chapter.
2. While the cabbage is steaming, dissolve the arrowroot in the ½ cup of water and cook over medium heat until mixture is clear and thickened.
3. Remove from the heat and add the vinegar, fructose, salt and caraway seeds; mix thoroughly.
4. Place the steamed cabbage in a mixing bowl. Pour the sauce over the cabbage and toss, mixing thoroughly.

Recipe continues . . .

Makes 8 servings.

Each serving contains approximately:
    ¼ fruit portion
    ½ vegetable portion
    23 calories
    0 mg. cholesterol
    42 mg. sodium

Mashed Potato Spoof

(It's really cauliflower!)

1 large head of cauliflower
1 tablespoon grated onion
¼ teaspoon salt
⅛ teaspoon white pepper
⅛ teaspoon ground nutmeg
¼ teaspoon fructose

1. Chop the cauliflower and cook in very little water until fork tender.
2. Mash cauliflower with a little of the water used for cooking.
3. Add all other ingredients and blend in a blender container or whip with an electric beater until fluffy.
4. Put the mixture in a casserole and bake at 350° for 20 minutes.

Makes 6 servings.

Each serving contains approximately:
    ½ vegetable portion
    12 calories
    0 mg. cholesterol
    54 mg. sodium

Nutty Wild Rice

½ cup chopped walnuts
4 ounces uncooked wild rice
  (¾ cup)
1½ cups Chicken Stock (see
  index)
2 teaspoons soy sauce

½ teaspoon dried thyme
½ teaspoon fructose
1 tablespoon corn oil margarine
1 large onion, chopped

1. Preheat the oven to 350°. Bake the walnuts in the oven for 10 to 15 minutes. Watch them carefully as they burn easily. Set aside.
2. Combine the wild rice, chicken stock, soy sauce, thyme and fructose in a saucepan with a lid.
3. Bring to a boil, reduce heat, cover, and simmer for 30 to 35 minutes, or until all the liquid is absorbed and the rice is fluffy. Remove from the heat and set aside.
4. Melt the margarine and add the chopped onion. Cook over medium heat until the onion is clear and tender.
5. Combine the cooked rice, toasted walnuts and cooked onion and mix well.

Makes 3 cups.

½ cup contains approximately:
    1 fat portion
    ¾ starch portion
    ¼ vegetable portion
    105 calories
    0 mg. cholesterol
    155 mg. sodium

109

Ravable Rice

2 tablespoons corn oil margarine
1 cup uncooked white rice
1 cup chopped tomatoes
1 pound fresh mushrooms,
sliced (4 cups)
½ cup finely chopped onion
3 cups Chicken Stock (see
index)

½ cup dry red wine
1½ teaspoons salt
1 teaspoon fructose
⅛ teaspoon freshly ground
black pepper
1 cup cooked green peas
¼ cup grated Parmesan cheese

1. Melt the margarine in a large skillet.
2. Add the rice, chopped tomatoes, sliced mushrooms and chopped onion. Cook, stirring occasionally, for about 10 minutes.
3. Add the chicken stock, wine, salt, fructose and pepper. Mix well.
4. Cover and simmer for about 45 minutes, or until the rice is tender and all of the liquid is absorbed
5. Stir in the peas and sprinkle Parmesan cheese on the top.
6. Cover and heat thoroughly.

Makes 6 servings.

Each serving contains approximately:
1 starch portion
1 fat portion
2 vegetable portions
165 calories
2.4 mg. cholesterol
528 mg. sodium

110

Fabulous Pilaf

3 tablespoons corn oil
1½ cups uncooked long-grain
  white rice
1 medium-size onion, thinly
  sliced

2 tablespoons soy sauce
1 teaspoon fructose
1 teaspoon dried thyme
2 cups Chicken Stock (see
  index)

1. Heat the oil in a skillet with nonstick coating and add the rice and onion slices to the heated oil.
2. Cook, stirring frequently, until browned thoroughly.
3. Add the soy sauce, fructose and thyme to the chicken stock and bring to the boiling point.
4. Put the rice mixture in a casserole dish with a tight-fitting lid and add the hot stock. Stir and cover.
5. Bake in a 400° oven for 40 minutes.
6. Remove from the oven and allow to stand for 10 minutes before removing lid.

To reheat: Add 2 or 3 tablespoons of chicken stock to the cold rice and mix thoroughly. Cover and heat slowly in a 300° oven for about 15 minutes.

Makes twelve ½-cup servings.

½ cup contains approximately:
  ½ starch portion
  ¾ fat portion
  72 calories
  0 mg cholesterol
  219 mg. sodium

Lemon Bulgur

(*Cracked Wheat*)

2 cups Chicken Stock (see index)
¼ teaspoon salt
½ teaspoon fructose
1 cup bulgur (cracked wheat)
2 teaspoons freshly grated lemon rind

1. Bring the chicken stock, salt and fructose to a boil.
2. Add the bulgur and bring back to a boil.
3. Cover and reduce the heat to low. Cook for 25 minutes.
4. Remove the lid, add the grated lemon rind, mix throughly, and allow bulgur to sit for 10 minutes before serving.

Makes 3 cups.

½ cup contains approximately:
    1 starch portion
    70 calories
    0 mg. cholesterol
    103 mg. sodium

Eggs and Cheese Dishes

The steadily rising number of vegetarians, combined with the high prices of meat in this country today, makes a meatless entrée section a very important part of a modern cookbook.

I also find that egg and cheese entrées provide greater latitude in menu planning than most meat dishes in that they are wonderful for brunches, luncheons and light suppers.

Many of the recipes in this section should serve as springboards for your imagination in creating new and unusual entrées of your own.

Eggplant Lasagna

1 can (20 ounces) tomatoes, drained and chopped
2 cans (6 ounces each) tomato paste
1 cup finely chopped fresh parsley
½ teaspoon salt
1 teaspoon fructose
¼ teaspoon freshly ground black pepper
1 teaspoon dried orégano

¼ teaspoon dried thyme
¼ teaspoon dried marjoram
2 onions, finely chopped
2 garlic cloves, finely chopped
2 large eggplants, peeled and sliced
2 cups ricotta cheese (½ pound)
2 cups grated mozarella cheese (½ pound)
1 cup grated Parmesan cheese

Recipe continues . . .

113

1. Combine all ingredients except eggplants and cheeses in a large saucepan and simmer, uncovered, for 30 minutes.
2. While the sauce is cooking, steam the eggplants according to directions on page 101.
3. Cover the bottom of a large flat baking dish with a thin layer of the tomato sauce. Place a layer of the steamed eggplant on top of it.
4. On top of the eggplant, place a layer of ricotta cheese, then a layer of mozarella, and then sprinkle with Parmesan cheese.
5. Repeat layers until the dish is filled. The top layer should be tomato sauce sprinkled with Parmesan cheese.
6. Bake in a preheated 350° oven for 30 minutes.

Makes 8 servings.

Each serving contains approximately:
>   4 medium-fat protein portions
>   1 vegetable portion
>   308 calories
>   37 mg. cholesterol
>   1052 mg. sodium

Swiss Fruit Fondue

4 slices of white bread
1 cup grated Swiss cheese (¼ pound)
2 large apples, peeled and thinly sliced
1 tablespoon fructose
1 teaspoon ground cinnamon
¼ teaspoon ground allspice
¼ teaspoon ground nutmeg
¼ teaspoon salt
1 teaspoon vanilla extract
4 eggs, lightly beaten
2 cups liquid nonfat milk

114

1. Allow the bread to stand out for several hours so that it can be easily cubed. Cut the bread in ¼-inch squares.
2. Arrange half of the bread in a flat baking dish.
3. Sprinkle half of the cheese over the bread.
4. Spread all of the sliced apples evenly over the cheese.
5. Put the remaining bread on top of the apples and the remaining cheese on top of the bread.
6. Combine all other ingredients and mix well. Pour the liquid mixture over the ingredients already in the baking dish. Cover and refrigerate overnight.
7. Remove from the refrigerator 2 hours before cooking.
8. To cook, set the baking dish in a layer pan with cold water to a depth of ¾ inch. Place in a preheated 300° oven and cook for 1 hour.

This may also be served as a dessert course after a very light meal.

Makes 4 servings.

Each serving contains approximately:
  1 high-fat protein portion
  1 medium-fat protein portion
  1 starch portion
  ½ nonfat milk portion
  1 fruit portion
  325 calories
  280 mg. cholesterol
  494 mg. sodium

Cheese Soufflé

1 cup liquid nonfat milk
4 teaspoons corn oil margarine
2½ tablespoons flour
4 egg yolks
1 teaspoon fructose
½ teaspoon salt
⅛ teaspoon freshly ground
black pepper
¼ teaspoon Worcestershire
sauce

½ cup grated cheese—Swiss,
Cheddar, Monterey Jack,
Romano, Parmesan or a
combination
5 egg whites, at room temperature
⅛ teaspoon cream of tartar

1. Preheat the oven to 400°.
2. Put the milk in a saucepan on low heat.
3. Put the margarine in another larger saucepan. Melt the margarine and add the flour, stirring constantly. Cook the flour and
butter for 3 minutes. *Do not brown!*
4. Take the flour-margarine mixture off the heat and pour in
the boiling milk, all at once, stirring with a wire whisk.
5. Put the pan back on the heat and allow sauce to come to a
boil, stirring constantly. Boil for 1 minute. At this point the
sauce will be quite thick. Remove from the heat.
6. Add the 4 egg yolks, one at a time, stirring each one in
throughly with a wire whisk.
7. Add the fructose, salt, pepper and Worcestershire sauce.
Stop! (You make this much of the soufflé ahead of time if you
are entertaining. Cover the saucepan; reheat the mixture to
lukewarm before adding the beaten egg whites. Or you can go
right ahead and finish the soufflé; it will be ready 20 to 25 minutes later; however, always remember you must wait for a soufflé because it will not wait for you.)
8. Add the cheese to the sauce and stir well.

116

9. Put the egg whites in a large mixing bowl. Add the cream of tartar. Beat the whites until stiff.

10. Add one fourth of the egg whites to the cheese sauce and stir them in. Add the remaining three fourths of the egg whites to the cheese sauce and very carefully fold them in, being sure not to overmix.

11. Spoon the mixture into an 8-inch soufflé dish and place in the center of the preheated 400° oven. Immediately reduce oven heat to 375°. Cook for 20 to 25 minutes. Serve immediately.

Makes 4 servings.

Each serving contains approximately:
    1½ medium-fat protein portions
    1 fat portion
    ¼ starch portion
    ¼ nonfat milk portion
    196 calories
    259 mg. cholesterol
    499 mg. sodium

English Pizza

2 English muffins
¼ cup Calorie-Cutter's Catsup (see index)
¼ teaspoon dried orégano
1 cup grated mozzarella or Monterey Jack cheese (¼ pound)
Freshly ground black pepper

1. Cut the muffins into halves and roll each half until it is flat and larger in diameter.
2. Spread each half with the catsup mixed with the orégano.
3. Sprinkle ¼ of the grated cheese on top of each half.
4. Place the muffins on a cookie sheet and bake in a 425° oven for 8 to 10 minutes, or until the cheese is bubbling and starting to brown.
5. To freeze: Put the pizzas on a cookie sheet; place under the broiler until the cheese just starts to melt. Cool, and place in individual plastic bags for storage in the freezer. To reheat, cook the same way as above, but for a couple of minutes longer.

These English Pizzas, with a salad, make a great lunch or dinner, and can be used for hors d'oeuvre.

Makes 4 servings.

Each serving contains approximately:
    1 starch portion
    1 high-fat protein portion
    165 calories
    17 mg. cholesterol
    400 mg. sodium

VARIATION: *You may add sliced mushrooms, chopped green pepper, chopped onion, anchovies, and many other things on top of the cheese for variety.*

Florentine Crêpes

2 pounds fresh spinach,
  chopped, or 2 packages
  (12 ounces each) frozen
  chopped spinach, thawed
1½ cups ricotta cheese
½ cup finely chopped green
  onions
¼ cup finely chopped fresh
  parsley

¼ teaspoon garlic powder
¼ teaspoon fructose
¼ teaspoon salt
8 crêpes (see index), warm
¼ cup grated Parmesan
  cheese

1. If you are using frozen chopped spinach, it is not necessary to steam it. If you are using fresh spinach, steam it according to the steaming directions on page 101. There should be 2 cups steamed.
2. Combine all ingredients except the crêpes and the Parmesan cheese in a large mixing bowl and mix well.
3. Spoon even amounts of the cheese-spinach mixture down the center of each crêpe.
4. Fold both sides of the crêpe over toward the center and place each crêpe seam side down in a glass baking dish.
5. Sprinkle the Parmesan cheese evenly over the tops of all of the crêpes.
6. Bake in a preheated 350° oven for 20 minutes, or until the Parmesan cheese is lightly browned.

Makes 8 crêpes.

Each crêpe contains approximately:
    ½ starch portion
    1 medium-fat protein portion
    ½ vegetable portion
    125 calories
    31.7 mg. cholesterol
    185 mg. sodium

119

Carrots à l'Indienne

2 tablespoons corn oil margarine
¼ teaspoon salt
½ teaspoon fructose
1 teaspoon curry powder
1 tablespoon freshly grated
  gingerroot, or ½ teaspoon
  ground ginger

6 medium-size carrots, grated
  (3 cups grated carrots)
¼ cup finely chopped chives
  or green onion tops
½ cup raisins
3 cups low-fat cottage cheese

1. Melt the corn oil margarine in a skillet.
2. Add the salt, fructose, curry powder and grated ginger and mix thoroughly.
3. Add the grated carrots, chopped chives and raisins and cook, stirring constantly, until just crisp-tender, about 10 minutes.
4. Add the cottage cheese, mix thoroughly, and heat just to serving temperature. *Do not bring to a boil!*

This deliciously different vegetarian entrée is very good served with Banana Bread (see index).

Makes 6 servings.

Each serving contains approximately:
  2 low-fat protein portions
  1 fat portion
  1 vegetable portion
  ¾ fruit portion
  210 calories
  5.2 mg. cholesterol
  610 mg. sodium

San Francisco Sourdough French Toast

4 eggs, or 1 cup liquid egg substitute
¼ cup buttermilk
¼ cup liquid nonfat milk
1 teaspoon fructose
6 slices of San Francisco sourdough bread (if using the extralarge slices, use 3 slices cut into halves)
1 tablespoon corn oil margarine

1. Beat the eggs, buttermilk, nonfat milk and fructose until well mixed.
2. Place the 6 slices of bread in a flat baking dish.
3. Pour the egg mixture over the bread. Pierce each slice of bread in several places with a fork to increase absorption of the egg mixture.
4. Cover the dish and place in the refrigerator (overnight if time permits).
5. When ready to cook, remove the bread from the baking dish and place it on an oiled cookie sheet, or one with nonstick coating, with sides. Pour any remaining liquid over the bread.
6. Place the bread under the broiler until golden brown in color. Turn the bread over and brown the other side.
7. Remove from the broiler and lightly spread with corn oil margarine, about ½ teaspoon per serving. Top with Strawberry Jam (see index) or whatever strikes your fancy, low calorie of course.

Makes 6 servings.

Each serving contains approximately:
    1 starch portion
    ¾ medium-fat protein portion
    ½ fat portion
    146 calories
    .7 mg. cholesterol with egg substitute
    168 mg. cholesterol with eggs
    306 mg. sodium

121

Eggs Foo Yung

2 cups bean sprouts, steamed according to directions on page 101.
½ cup finely chopped chives or green onion tops
8 eggs, lightly beaten
2 teaspoons corn oil

Sauce:
> 3 tablespoons soy sauce
> 1 tablespoon cornstarch
> 4 teaspoons cider vinegar
> 1 teaspoon fructose
> ¾ cup water

1. To make the egg foo yung patties, combine the steamed bean sprouts, chopped chives and lightly beaten eggs and mix well.
2. Heat the oil in a large skillet. When the oil is hot, spoon out the egg mixture like pancakes, using about ¼ cup per patty.
3. When lightly browned on one side, turn over and brown the other side. Then turn the heat as low as possible until the egg is completely done, about 5 minutes. Serve with a little sauce over the top of each patty.
4. To make the sauce, combine all ingredients in a saucepan and stir until the cornstarch is completely dissolved. Cook over low heat, stirring constantly, until thickened.

Makes 4 servings.

Each serving contains approximately:
> 2 medium-fat protein portions
> ¼ starch portion
> ½ fat portion

122

191 calories
504 mg. cholesterol
899 mg. sodium

Fettuccine alla Fabulosa

4 cups cooked Fettuccine
 Pasta (see index)
4 tablespoons corn oil margarine
¼ teaspoon garlic powder

½ teaspoon fructose
½ cup freshly grated Romano
 cheese
¼ teaspoon freshly ground
 black pepper

1. While the pasta is cooking, melt the margarine and add the garlic powder and fructose, mixing throughly.
2. When the pasta is ready, pour it into a colander or large strainer and drain well.
3. Pour the pasta into a bowl, pour the garlic mixture over it and mix thoroughly.
4. Add the Romano cheese and pepper and again mix well. Serve at once.

Makes 8 servings.

Each serving contains approximately:
   ¼ medium-fat protein portion
   1 starch portion
   2¼ fat portions
   190 calories
   4 mg. cholesterol
   219 mg. sodium

Huevos Rancheros

2 teaspoons corn oil
1 onion, chopped
1 green bell pepper, seeded
and chopped
2 garlic cloves, pressed
3½ cups canned peeled tomatoes (one 28-ounce can),
chopped, with the juice
from the can
3 green chilies, chopped, with
ribs and seeds removed

1 teaspoon salt
1 teaspoon fructose
½ teaspoon freshly ground
black pepper
1 teaspoon chili powder
1 teaspoon dried orégano
½ teaspoon ground cuminseed
6 eggs, at room temperature
1½ cups grated Monterey Jack
cheese
6 corn tortillas, hot

1. Heat the corn oil in a skillet with nonstick coating.
2. Add the onion, green bell pepper and garlic. Cook until the onion is clear.
3. Add all other ingredients except the eggs, cheese and tortillas, and cook for 20 minutes.
4. Place the eggs on the top of the sauce, making a little depression for each egg. Sprinkle the grated cheese all over the top.
5. Cover and cook for 3 to 5 minutes, or until the egg whites are white and the cheese is melted.
6. Serve each egg on top of a hot tortilla, spooning the remaining sauce over the top of each serving.

Makes 6 servings.

Each serving contains approximately:
2 medium-fat protein portions
1 starch portion
½ fat portion
1 vegetable portion
268 calories
277 mg. cholesterol
652 mg. sodium

124

Strawberry Jam Omelet

2 eggs
1 tablespoon water
Dash of salt
Dash of pepper
½ teaspoon corn oil margarine

⅓ cup Strawberry Jam (see
index), or a commercial
fructose-sweetened product
(see Appendix 4)

1. Beat eggs with a fork until frothy.
2. Add 1 tablespoon water, salt and pepper and beat again.
3. Meanwhile, melt the margarine in an omelet pan or skillet with nonstick coating (skillet should have slanted sides) until sizzling hot. Reduce the heat and pour in the beaten egg. The egg will immediately start to set.
4. Using a fork, scrape the set edges of the egg toward the center, tilting the pan at the same time so that the egg liquid then seeps underneath to cook.
5. When the bottom is cooked but the top is still runny, place the Strawberry Jam in a strip across the center. Fold over one third of the omelet toward the center.
6. Rest the edge of the pan on the plate and quickly turn the pan upside down, so the omelet, folded in thirds, slides out on the plate.

Makes 1 serving.

1 omelet contains approximately:
    2 medium-fat protein portions
    ½ fat portion
    1 fruit portion
    213 calories
    504 mg. cholesterol
    319 mg. sodium

Dieter's Dream Quiche

Crust:

1 cup whole-wheat flour
¼ teaspoon salt

¼ cup corn oil
3 tablespoons ice water

Quiche:

3 cups grated Swiss
cheese (¾ pound)
½ cup grated Parmesan
cheese
3 eggs, beaten
1¼ cups low-fat millk
¼ cup tomato sauce
¼ teaspoon salt

¼ teaspoon white pepper
¼ teaspoon fructose
¼ teaspoon ground nut-
meg, crushed
¼ teaspoon dried orégano
¼ teaspoon dried sweet
basil, crushed

1. Put the flour and salt in a 9-inch pie pan or quiche dish and mix well. (I always make the crust in a 9-inch quiche dish.)
2. Measure the oil in a large measuring cup. Add the water to the oil and mix well, using a fork.
3. Slowly add the liquid to the flour mixture in the pie pan or quiche dish, mixing it with the same fork. Continue mixing until all ingredients are well blended.
4. Press into shape with your fingers. Make sure that the crust covers the entire inner surface of the pan evenly. Set aside.
5. Preheat the oven to 350°.
6. Layer the Swiss cheese and Parmesan cheese in the unbaked pie shell. Start with 1 cup of grated Swiss cheese, then ¼ cup of Parmesan. Follow with 1 more cup of Swiss, then the remaining Parmesan. Sprinkle the remaining cup of Swiss cheese evenly over the top.
7. Beat the eggs with the milk and tomato sauce. Add all other ingredients and mix well.

126

8. Pour this mixture over the cheese in the pie shell. Place the quiche on a cookie sheet so that if it bubbles up during baking the drips will go on the cookie sheet rather than the bottom of the oven.

9. Bake in the preheated oven for 1 hour. Remove from the oven and allow to cool for 10 minutes before cutting to serve.

If you wish to freeze the quiche, cool to room temperature and wrap tightly in aluminum foil. To reheat, remove from the freezer 3 to 4 hours before reheating. Then heat in a 350° oven for about 15 minutes.

This quiche makes an excellent brunch or light supper entrée. It is also good cut into small pieces and served as hors d'oeuvre.

Makes 8 servings.

Each serving contains approximately:
   1 starch portion
   3 medium-fat protein portions
   1 fat portion
   316 calories
   143 mg. cholesterol
   333 mg. sodium

Fish and Shellfish

Fish is one of the best sources of protein in our diet because it contains less fat and fewer calories than other animal proteins.

If you don't think you like fish, you have probably never had it prepared properly; or you have never had really fresh fish; or maybe both.

Modern transportation makes it possible to buy fresh fish almost everywhere. When it is impossible to buy fresh fish, buy frozen fish and thaw it slowly in cold water, and then prepare it in exactly the same manner that you would fresh fish.

Never cook fish while it is still frozen because it has practically no taste and will have a mushy consistency.

Fish Preparation

1. Wash fish in cold water and pat dry.
2. Squeeze lemon juice over both sides of the fish.
3. Lightly sprinkle fructose over both sides of the fish.
4. Cover tightly with a lid or aluminum foil and place in the refrigerator until you are ready to cook it. If you are planning to cook the fish soon after purchasing it, it will not be necessary to refrigerate it before cooking.

128

Allowing the fish to stand in the lemon juice takes away the "fishy" taste many people find objectionable. I use fructose, either granular or liquid, in preference to salt because I think it better heightens the flavor of all other seasonings you plan to use in preparing the fish. Also it is one place where sodium can be lowered for people on sodium restricted diets without anyone else missing the salt.

Baked Salmon

2 cups cooked salmon, or 1 pound canned salmon, drained
2 eggs, lightly beaten
1 cup liquid nonfat milk
2 tablespoons finely chopped capers
2 tablespoons finely chopped onion

2 tablespoons lemon juice
1 teaspoon fructose
⅛ teaspoon freshly ground black pepper
½ teaspoon Worcestershire sauce

1. Mix all the ingredients together and pour into a loaf pan.
2. Bake at 350° for 35 minutes, or until firm.
3. Serve hot with a green salad, or serve cold with marinated cold vegetables. Also try it cold as a sandwich spread.

Makes 4 servings.

Each serving contains approximately:
    2½ low-fat protein portions
    ¼ low-fat milk portion
    170 calories
    126 mg. cholesterol
    804 mg. sodium

Herbed Fish Amandine

2 pounds boneless red snapper, or any firm fish
¼ cup finely chopped almonds
½ cup Mayonnaise (see
index), or commercial
fructose-sweetened mayon-
naise (see Appendix 4)

1 cup plain low-fat yogurt
½ teaspoon salt
½ teaspoon fructose
1 teaspoon dried tarragon,
crushed
1½ teaspoons dill weed,
crushed

1. Prepare the fish according to directions given at the beginning of this chapter.
2. Bake the almonds in a 350° oven for 8 to 10 minutes, or until
golden brown. Watch them carefully as they burn easily. Set
aside.
3. When you are ready to cook the fish, remove from the refrigerator, allowing enough time for the dish to come to room temperature so that it will not break in the oven.
4. Place the tightly covered baking dish in a 350° oven for 15
minutes (a little longer if the fish is extremely thick). Remove
the dish from the oven and pour off all excess liquid.
5. Put the mayonnaise, yogurt, salt and fructose in a mixing
bowl and mix thoroughly, using a wire whisk.
6. Crush the tarragon and dill weed thoroughly, using a mortar
and pestle. Add the crushed herbs to the other sauce ingredients and mix thoroughly. (This sauce is even better if it is
made 2 days in advance and kept in the refrigerator.)
7. Spoon the sauce evenly over the fish. Sprinkle almonds
evenly on top of each serving.

Makes 8 servings.

Each serving contains approximately:
    3 low-fat protein portions

1½ fat portions
233 calories
71 mg. cholesterol
292 mg. sodium

Cooper's Crispies

1 can (6 ounces) water-packed
    tuna or salmon, drained
¼ cup finely chopped celery
1 egg, lightly beaten
½ teaspoon lemon juice

½ teaspoon liquid fructose
⅛ teaspoon garlic powder
1 teaspoon Worcestershire
    sauce

1. Combine all ingredients and mix well.
2. Shape into 2 equal-size patties.
3. Spray a large skillet with a nonstick spray and heat the skillet.
4. Place the 2 patties in the skillet and cook until crispy brown on both sides.

    This recipe is only a slight modification of the tuna crispies in Dr. Cooper's first book, *Fabulous Fructose Diet*. Because this particular recipe has been an ongoing source of amusement for both of us, I decided to change it slightly and use it again. In modifying his original recipe I have also reduced greatly the amount of sodium in the crispies.

Makes 2 crispies.

Each crispy contains approximately:
    3 low-fat protein portions
    ½ medium-fat protein portion
    205 calories
    126 mg. cholesterol
    590 mg. sodium

131

Bass Buffet Platter

2 pounds boneless fresh
striped bass or white sea
bass
1 onion, chopped
2 celery stalks, chopped
2 carrots, sliced
1 bunch of fresh parsley,
stems and leaves, chopped
½ teaspoon salt
½ teaspoon fructose

⅛ teaspoon white pepper
2 cups dry white wine
1 envelope unflavored gelatin
3 tablespoons water
2 bay leaves
½ cup Mayonnaise (see
index), or a commercial
fructose-sweetened mayon-
naise (see Appendix 4)
½ cup minced fresh parsley

Optional for garnish:
Reserved vegetables
from poaching liquid
Parsley sprigs
Tomato wedges
Capers (Use your imagi-
nation!)

1. Prepare the fish according to directions given at the beginning of this chapter. Put the fish in a large saucepan.
2. Add the onion, celery, carrots and chopped parsley.
3. Mix the salt, fructose and pepper with the wine and pour over all of the ingredients in the saucepan. If the wine doesn't cover completely, add a little more wine.
4. Bring to a simmer and cover. Cook for 8 to 10 minutes, or until the fish turns white.
5. Remove from the heat and allow to come to room temperature.
6. Remove the fish from the poaching liquid and arrange on a serving platter, reserving the liquid. Cover the platter tightly

132

with aluminum foil or plastic wrap and place in the refrigerator.

7. Soften the gelatin in the 3 tablespoons of water.

8. Put the poaching liquid back on the heat and bring to a boil. Strain the hot liquid, reserving 1¾ cups. Refrigerate the vegetables to serve later with the fish.

9. Add the softened gelatin to the 1¾ cups of hot liquid and mix until the gelatin is thoroughly dissolved.

10. Add the bay leaves and allow the mixture to cool to room temperature; then cover it and place in the refrigerator for about 1 hour, or until it is slightly jelled.

11. At this point, remove the bay leaves and add the mayonnaise to the gelatin mixture, mixing thoroughly with a wire whisk.

12. Remove the cold platter of fish from the refrigerator. Spoon the gelatin-mayonnaise mixture evenly over the entire fish platter.

13. Sprinkle the minced parsley evenly over the top. Re-cover the platter of fish and put back in the refrigerator until firmly jelled. Garnish as desired.

I call this Bass Buffet Platter because it looks so pretty, with garnish, on a buffet table, and it is so easy to serve.

Makes 8 servings.

Each serving contains approximately:
    3 low-fat protein portions
    3 fat portions
    300 calories
    83 mg. cholesterol
    248 mg. sodium

Tuna in Tartar Sauce

2 cans (7 ounces each) water-
  packed tuna, drained
4 slices of whole-wheat bread,
  toasted and crumbled
1 cup Tartar Sauce (see
  index)

1 jar (2 ounces) pimientos,
  thinly sliced
1 tablespoon capers, drained
Parsley sprigs for garnish

1. Combine tuna, bread and tartar sauce; mix well, and place in a glass baking dish 7 × 11 inches.
2. Press down with a spoon and decorate the top with sliced pimientos and capers.
3. Bake in a 350° oven for 15 to 20 minutes.
4. Garnish with sprigs of parsley. Sliced tomatoes and a green vegetable are good accompaniments to this entrée.

Makes 6 servings.

Each serving contains approximately:
  2 low-fat protein portions
  3 fat portions
  ¾ starch portion
  298 calories
  16 mg. cholesterol
  315 mg. sodium

Oysters Rockefeller Casserole

1 jar (16 ounces) fresh oysters (or 16 fresh oysters, shelled)
1 pound fresh spinach, chopped (3½ cups), or 2 packages (10 ounces each) frozen chopped spinach, thawed
2 cups Mornay Sauce (see index)
1 tablespoon grated Romano cheese

1. Steam the spinach in accordance with the directions on page 101 and set aside.
2. Pour the juice from the oysters into a large skillet.
3. Add the oysters and cook until the edges curl and the oysters turn white, about 5 minutes.
4. Line the bottom of a glass baking dish 12 × 8 inches with the spinach.
5. Arrange the oysters on top of the spinach and pour the juice from the pan evenly over the top.
6. Spoon the Mornay sauce evenly over the top of the entire baking dish, and, sprinkle with Romano cheese.
7. Bake in a preheated 350° oven for 10 minutes. Lightly brown under a broiler before serving.

Makes 4 servings.

Each serving contains approximately:
    1½ low-fat protein portions
    ¾ fat portion
    ½ nonfat milk portion
    ¼ starch portion
    217 calories
    97 mg. cholesterol
    727 mg. sodium

Cioppino

4 teaspoons corn oil
1 large onion, chopped
8 whole green onions, tops included
1 green bell pepper, seeded and chopped
2 garlic cloves, whole
½ cup minced parsley
1 can (16 ounces) tomato purée
1 can (8 ounces) tomato sauce
1 cup water

1 cup dry white wine
1 bay leaf
⅛ teaspoon dried rosemary
⅛ teaspoon dried thyme
1 teaspoon salt
1 teaspoon fructose
¼ teaspoon freshly ground black pepper
2 medium-size crabs, cracked
16 clams in the shells
1 pound large shrimps or prawns in the shells

1. Heat the oil in a large pot or soup kettle.
2. Cook the onion, green onions, green bell pepper and garlic until the onion is clear but not browned, about 5 minutes.
3. Add the parsley, tomato purée, tomato sauce, water, wine and all seasonings. Cover and simmer for 1 hour.
4. Break the crabs into pieces. Scrub the clams with a brush, making sure all sand is removed. Cut the shrimps down the back with scissors, wash and remove veins.
5. Remove the garlic from the pot. Add the crabs first, then the clams and shrimps.
6. Cook, covered, until the clams are open and the shrimps turn pink, about 8 minutes.

Serve with a tossed green salad and sourdough bread. Bibs for your guests are a good idea. Cioppino is delicious, fun to eat, but messy.

Makes 8 servings.

Each serving contains approximately:
    3½ low-fat protein portions

½ fat portion
1 vegetable portion
241 calories
102 mg. cholesterol
1559 mg. sodium

New England Clams and Vegetables

2 teaspoons corn oil margarine
2 cans (8 ounces each)
   chopped clams, undrained
2 garlic cloves, finely chopped
4 large zucchini squash, sliced

½ cup minced fresh parsley
¼ cup finely chopped fresh
   chives or green onion tops
¼ cup grated Parmesan
   cheese

1. Melt the margarine in a large skillet.
2. Add the juice from both cans of clams and the garlic to the melted margarine.
3. Add the sliced zucchini to the clam juice and cook until tender, about 5 minutes.
4. Add half of the parsley and the chives and cook for 5 minutes more.
5. Add the chopped clams, Parmesan cheese and remaining ¼ cup of parsley. Mix well and serve at once.
   Overcooking the clams will make them tough.

Makes 4 servings.

Each serving contains approximately:
   1 low-fat protein portion
   1 vegetable portion
   ½ fat portion
   103 calories
   71 mg. cholesterol
   309 mg. sodium

Poultry

I like to use poultry of all types when I am working on new recipes. Poultry lends itself to the total range of flavors and seasonings better than red meats and it is also lower in fat content and calories.

Roast Chicken

1 whole roasting chicken
1 tablespoon liquid fructose
1 tablespoon fresh lemon juice

1. Preheat the oven to 350°.
2. Put the chicken, breast side down, in a flat roasting pan.
3. Combine the fructose and lemon juice and rub the mixture over the entire outer surface of the chicken.
4. Bake at 350° for 1 hour, or until the liquid from the chicken runs clear.
5. If you are going to use the chicken for salad, allow to cool before skinning and cutting into smaller pieces.

1 slice, 3 x 2 x ⅛ inch, or 1 ounce, or ¼ cup chopped contains approximately:

138

1 low-fat protein portion
55 calories
28 mg. cholesterol
22 mg. sodium

VARIATION: *If you wish herbs or spices to season your chicken, combine them with the fructose and lemon juice before rubbing it on the chicken. I often add 1 teaspoon of curry powder and ¼ teaspoon of ground ginger.*

Turkish Turkey

2 cups plain low-fat yogurt
½ cup freshly squeezed lemon
   juice
1 tablespoon ground cuminseed
1 teaspoon salt

½ teaspoon freshly ground
   black pepper
3 garlic cloves, minced
1 pound cooked turkey (4
   slices without skin)

1. Combine all ingredients except the turkey and mix well.
2. Place the turkey in a glass baking dish. Pour the sauce over the turkey.
3. Cover and bake in a 350° oven for approximately 30 minutes.

Makes 4 servings.

Each serving contains approximately:
    4 low-fat protein portions
    ½ nonfat milk portion
    280 calories
    106 mg. cholesterol
    699 mg. sodium

Roast Turkey

1 turkey
1 tablespoon corn oil
2 tablespoons liquid fructose
2 tablespoons fresh lemon juice

1. Preheat the oven to 325°.
2. Put the turkey, breast down, in a flat roasting pan.
3. Combine the corn oil, liquid fructose and lemon juice.
4. Rub the entire outer surface of the turkey with the oil mixture. Put it in the oven and cook for 20 minutes per pound.
5. Take the turkey from the oven, allow it to cool slightly, and put it on a platter.
6. Pour the turkey drippings into a bowl and put in the freezer.
7. When the fat has solidified on the top (about 30 minutes), scrape it off and use the defatted drippings for gravy with your turkey dinner or store them in the refrigerator to use in turkey soup.

1 slice, 3 x 2 x ⅛ inch, without skin, or 1 ounce, or ¼ cup chopped, contains approximately:
    1 low-fat protein portion
    55 calories
    22 mg. cholesterol
    23 mg. sodium

VARIATION: *If you wish herbs or spices to season your turkey, combine them with the fructose and lemon juice before rubbing it on the turkey. I often add 1 tablespoon of dried thyme, tarragon, or rosemary. I also like to stuff the turkey with onion and garlic.*

140

Chinese Chicken and Snow Peas

3 whole chicken breasts,
cooked
1 tablespoon corn oil
½ pound bean sprouts
½ pound Chinese pea pods
(snow peas)
1 cup chopped green onions
2 cups sliced fresh
mushrooms

1 cup Chicken Stock (see
index)
2 tablespoons soy sauce
1 teaspoon grated peeled
gingerroot
½ teaspoon salt
1 teaspoon fructose
1½ tablespoons cornstarch
2 tablespoons cold water

1. Remove the skin, fat and bones from the chicken breasts.
Cut the chicken breasts into ½-inch strips. Set aside.
2. Heat the oil in a large skillet. Cook the bean sprouts, pea
pods, green onions and mushrooms in the same skillet just a
few minutes, until crisp-tender.
3. Add the chicken stock, soy sauce, ginger, salt and fructose.
Cover and cook for 2 minutes.
4. Stir in the cornstarch mixed with the cold water. Cook, stirring, until clear and slightly thickened.
5. Add the chicken strips and mix well. Serve over white rice.

Makes 6 servings.

Each serving contains approximately:
    2 low-fat protein portions
    ½ fat portion
    1¼ vegetable portions
    164 calories
    83 mg. cholesterol
    656 mg. sodium

Recipe continues . . .

½ cup cooked white rice contains approximately:
    1 starch portion
    70 calories
    0 mg. cholesterol
    3 mg. sodium

Chicken Enchilada Torte

1 tablespoon corn oil
1 large onion, finely chopped
1 can (16 ounces) whole tomatoes, undrained
1 tablespoon chili powder
1 teaspoon salt
½ teaspoon ground cuminseed

½ teaspoon fructose
Dash of Tabasco
2 cups chopped cooked chicken without skin
1½ cups grated sharp Cheddar cheese
8 corn tortillas, warm

1. Preheat the oven to 350°.
2. Heat the oil in a large skillet.
3. Add the chopped onion and cook until tender.
4. While the onion is cooking, remove the tomatoes from the can, reserving the juice to add later. Chop the tomatoes and add to the cooked onion in the skillet.
5. Combine the reserved tomato juice with the chili powder, salt, cuminseed, fructose and Tabasco; mix well.
6. Pour the liquid mixture into the skillet with the onion and tomatoes; add the chopped cooked chicken and mix well.
7. Cook, uncovered, over low heat for 5 minutes.
8. Add 1 cup of the grated Cheddar cheese to the mixture in the skillet and mix well.
9. To make the enchilada torte, spoon enough of the chicken mixture into the bottom of a round 3-quart casserole to cover the bottom to a depth of ¼ inch. Place a tortilla on top of the chicken mixture and continue to layer the enchilada filling and

the tortillas, spreading filling evenly over each tortilla, until all of the tortillas and all of the sauce have been placed in the casserole. The top layer should be the sauce.

10. Sprinkle the remaining ½ cup of grated cheese over the top of the torte.

11. Cover the baking dish with a lid or aluminum foil and bake in the 350° oven for 30 minutes.

12. To serve, slice the torte, as you would a pie, into 6 pieces and serve on a plate.

This is a delicious entrée which can be made ahead of time and heated before serving. Enchilada Tortes are wonderful for Mexican dinner parties. They can easily be served for a buffet. I like to serve Gazpacho as the first course and fresh fruit for dessert.

Makes 6 servings.

Each serving contains approximately:
  1 starch portion
  1 vegetable portion
  2 low-fat protein portions
  1 fat portion
  255 calories
  61.6 mg. cholesterol
  268 mg. sodium

Chicken Curry

3 tablespoons corn oil margarine
3 onions, finely chopped
5 tablespoons flour
2 tablespoons curry powder
1 teaspoon fructose
½ teaspoon salt

¼ teaspoon ground ginger
1 cup Chicken Stock (see index)
3 cups liquid nonfat milk, warmed
1½ pounds cooked chicken (6 cups)

Recipe continues . . .

143

1. In a large pot melt the margarine.
2. Add the finely chopped onions and cook until the onions are clear and tender.
3. Combine the flour, curry powder, fructose, salt and ground ginger.
4. Add the flour mixture to the onions, stirring constantly, until mixture becomes a thick paste.
5. Add the chicken stock and stir until mixture again becomes a thick paste.
6. Slowly add the warm milk, stirring constantly. Cook slowly, stirring regularly, until the sauce has thickened, about 45 minutes. It never gets very thick.
7. Add the chicken and heat thoroughly. Serve over plain white rice.

Makes 8 servings.

Each serving contains approximately:
   2¼ low-fat protein portions
   1 fat portion
   1 vegetable portion
   ¼ starch portion
   210 calories
   71 mg. cholesterol
   293 mg. sodium
½ cup cooked white rice contains approximately:
   1 starch portion
   70 calories
   0 mg. cholesterol
   3 mg. sodium

Pizza Chicken

2 cups tomato juice
2 tablespoons red-wine vinegar
¼ teaspoon salt
½ teaspoon fructose
1 medium onion, thinly sliced
1 teaspoon dried orégano
4 whole chicken breasts,
boned, halved, skinned and
  all visible fat removed
1 tablespoon corn oil margarine
Freshly ground black pepper
½ cup Chicken Stock (see
  index)
1 cup grated mozzarella
  cheese

1. Put the tomato juice in a large saucepan. Add the vinegar, salt, fructose and onion and mix thoroughly.
2. Bring the mixture to a boil and reduce the heat. Simmer, uncovered, for 1 hour.
3. Add the orégano and continue to simmer, uncovered, for 30 minutes.
4. Preheat the oven to 400°.
5. Put the chicken breasts in a baking dish large enough not to overlap them. Rub a little corn oil margarine evenly on each piece of chicken, then sprinkle salt and freshly ground black pepper over the tops.
6. Pour the chicken stock into the baking dish.
7. Cover the dish tightly with a lid or aluminum foil and place it in the preheated oven for 20 minutes.
8. Remove the chicken from the oven and pour off the liquid.
9. Spread the tomato sauce evenly over the chicken; leave chicken uncovered. Return dish to the oven for 10 minutes.
10. Remove dish from the oven and sprinkle the grated cheese evenly over the chicken.
11. Place chicken under the broiler until the cheese is melted and lightly browned.

Recipe continues . . .

Serve Pizza Chicken with a tossed green salad, Fettuccine Alla Fabulosa and fresh fruit for dessert.

Makes 8 servings.

Each serving contains approximately:
  ¾ vegetable portion
  2 low-fat protein portions
  ½ medium-fat protein portion
  190 calories
  92 mg. cholesterol
  421 mg. sodium

Game Hens alla Cacciatora

6 Cornish game hens
2 medium onions, peeled and diced
1 can (16 ounces) Italian tomatoes
2 garlic cloves, minced
4 teaspoons dried rosemary
1½ teaspoons dried orégano
1 teaspoon olive oil
1 teaspoon corn oil

2 teaspoons liquid fructose
Salt
1 can (6 ounces) tomato paste
1½ cups dry white wine (I like Chablis)
½ cup dry Marsala wine
1 tablespoon corn oil margarine
¾ pound fresh mushrooms, thinly sliced (3 cups)

1. Preheat the oven to 350°.
2. Wash the game hens well, both inside and out, and pat dry.
3. Combine the diced onions, tomatoes, garlic, 3 teaspoons rosemary and the orégano and mix well. Stuff half of the mixture into each game hen.
4. Combine the olive oil, corn oil, fructose and remaining rosemary and mix well.

5. Rub the game hens with the oil mixture and sprinkle each game hen lightly with salt.

6. Place the game hens in a baking dish or roasting pan in which they fit closely together. Bake them in the preheated oven for 15 minutes.

7. While the game hens are cooking, combine the tomato paste, white wine and Marsala, and mix thoroughly. Pour the wine mixture over the top of the game hens and continue to bake for 45 more minutes, basting frequently.

8. While the game hens are continuing to cook, melt the corn oil margarine in a large skillet. Add the sliced mushrooms and cook until just tender.

9. Remove the game hens from the oven and place them on individual serving plates or a platter.

10. Combine the sauce and sautéed mushrooms and mix well; spoon evenly over the top of the game hens. Garnish with fresh parsley if available.

If you wish to cook the game hens ahead of time, reheat them in a 400° oven for 15 minutes. I routinely prepare my game hens ahead of time and reheat them before serving because I think it improves their flavor.

Makes 6 servings.

Each serving contains approximately:
> 4 low-fat protein portions
> 2 vegetable portions
> 1 fat portion
> 315 calories
> 92 mg. cholesterol
> 216 mg. sodium

Meat

Red meats are higher in fat content and calories than fish and poultry. For this reason it is best to limit the number of times per week you serve red meat when you are on a diet for weight reduction or weight maintenance; *and you should always be on a diet for weight maintenance.*

I have included in this section only my own favorite recipes using red meat. I do not eat it very often myself; and therefore I want to save the times I do eat it for something I particularly like.

Hawaiian Pineapple Meat Loaf

1 teaspoon corn oil
3 large onions, thinly sliced
3 pounds lean ground beef
   round
1 teaspoon salt
¼ teaspoon white pepper
1 can (20 ounces) crushed

pineapple packed in natural
   juice, drained
1 tablespoon liquid fructose
¼ teaspoon ground cinnamon
¼ teaspoon ground nutmeg
¼ teaspoon ground allspice
2 cups cooked rice

1. Heat the corn oil in a large skillet over medium heat.
2. Add the onions and cook, stirring frequently, for 30 minutes.

3. Reduce the heat and continue cooking until the onions are browned.

4. While the onions are cooking, place the meat in a large mixing bowl, add all other ingredients, and mix well.

5. When the onions are browned and cooled to room temperature, add the onions to the meat mixture and again mix thoroughly.

6. Shape the meat into a large loaf and place it in a baking dish.

7. Place the meat loaf in a preheated 350° oven and bake for 1 hour.

Makes 12 servings.

Each serving contains approximately:
    1 vegetable portion
    3 medium-fat protein portions
    ½ fruit portion
    ½ starch portion
    305 calories
    105 mg. cholesterol
    248 mg. sodium

Ham Slices in Orange Sauce

4 slices of cooked ham (½ pound)
Paprika
1½ teaspoons cornstarch
½ cup orange juice
¼ teaspoon salt

½ teaspoon ground cinnamon
⅛ teaspoon ground cloves
2 tablespoons fructose
2 teaspoons grated orange rind
1 orange, thinly sliced

Recipe continues . . .

149

1. Trim all the fat from the ham slices.
2. Sprinkle both sides of each slice with paprika.
3. In a skillet with nonstick coating, lightly brown the ham on both sides.
4. In a saucepan, mix the cornstarch with the orange juice, and add the salt, cinnamon, cloves, fructose and orange rind.
5. Cook over low heat until clear and slightly thickened.
6. Pour the orange sauce over the ham slices and garnish with orange slices.

Makes 4 servings.

Each serving contains approximately:
    2 low-fat protein portions
    1 fruit portion
    150 calories
    51 mg. cholesterol
    823 mg. sodium

Fabulous Stew

1½ pounds lean beef, cut into 1-inch cubes
½ cup flour
1 tablespoon corn oil margarine
2 onions, coarsely chopped
½ pound fresh mushrooms, sliced (2 cups)
2 parsley sprigs, minced
2 garlic cloves, minced
2 bay leaves (remove when cooked)
½ teaspoon salt
1 teaspoon fructose
½ teaspoon freshly ground black pepper
½ teaspoon dill weed
½ teaspoon dried summer savory
½ teaspoon dried thyme
1½ cups water
2 cups dry red wine
1 carrot, sliced
2 turnips, cut into large pieces
2 cups green peas

1. Put cubed beef and flour in a paper bag and shake until the meat is thoroughly coated with flour.
2. Melt the margarine in the bottom of a soup kettle. Add the onions and mushrooms, sauté until tender, and remove from the pan. Do not wash the pan.
3. Add the meat to the hot pan and brown rapidly.
4. When the meat is brown, return the onions and mushrooms to the pan. Add the parsley and all other herbs and seasonings.
5. Add ½ cup water and 1 cup of the wine. Simmer, covered, for 45 minutes.
6. Add the remaining cup of water and cup of wine, and simmer for another 30 minutes.
7. Cool and refrigerate overnight.
8. Chip off all fat from the top. When reheating, bring to a slow boil and add all of the vegetables except the peas.
9. Simmer, covered, for 1 hour. Add peas and cook until they are tender, about 10 minutes.

Makes 8 servings.

Each serving contains approximately:
>   2 low-fat protein portions
>   1 vegetable portion
>   ½ fat portion
>   1 starch portion
>   228 calories
>   75 mg. cholesterol
>   222 mg. sodium

Shashlik

1 pound lean lamb, cut into cubes
1 green bell pepper
12 small boiling onions
12 cherry tomatoes

Marinade:
½ cup red-wine vinegar
2 tablespoons soy sauce
¼ teaspoon freshly ground black pepper
Dash of cayenne pepper
1 teaspoon salt
1 teaspoon fructose
½ cup minced onion
1 tablespoon dried orégano

1. Combine all ingredients for the marinade and marinate lamb cubes for 8 hours.
2. Wash the green pepper and cut into 1-inch squares, removing all seeds and ribs.
3. Peel the onions and parboil for 3 minutes.
4. Arrange the cubes of marinated lamb on skewers, alternating the lamb cubes with the cherry tomatoes, green pepper squares and onions.
5. Put the skewers back in the marinade for 1 to 2 hours.
6. Broil in the oven or over a charcoal fire until the lamb is cooked the desired amount.

Makes 6 servings.

Each serving contains approximately:
2 low-fat protein portions

1 vegetable portion
135 calories
65 mg. cholesterol
585 mg. sodium

Dieter's Spicy Sausage

2 pounds ground lean pork
(absolutely all fat removed
before grinding.)
2 teaspoons ground sage
1 teaspoon freshly ground
black pepper
1 teaspoon fructose

¾ teaspoon garlic powder
½ teaspoon onion powder
½ teaspoon ground mace
¼ teaspoon ground allspice
¼ teaspoon salt
⅛ teaspoon ground cloves

1. Combine all ingredients in a large mixing bowl and mix thoroughly.
2. Form into 12 sausage patties. Cook in a nonstick pan until slightly browned on both sides.

I often double this recipe and freeze the sausage patties in individual plastic bags. The flavor improves if they are made a day or two before you plan to cook them. Dieter's Spicy Sausage patties are not only much lower in calories than any other sausage, but I think they are even more delicious.

Makes 12 patties.

Each patty contains approximately:
2 medium-fat protein portions
150 calories
58 mg. cholesterol
89 mg. sodium

153

Cantonese Sweet-and-Sour Pork

1 pound lean pork roast,
  cooked
1 can (20 ounces) unsweetened pineapple chunks
  with juice
2 tablespoons cornstarch
⅓ cup cider vinegar
3 tablespoons fructose

2 tablespoons soy sauce
¼ pound fresh mushrooms,
  sliced (1 cup)
1 green bell pepper, seeded
  and thinly sliced
1 onion, thinly sliced
1 can (6 ounces) water chestnuts, thinly sliced

1. Cut the roast pork into 1-inch cubes, making sure to remove all fat. There should be 4 cups of cubes.
2. Drain the juice from the pineapple chunks and pour it into a large saucepan.
3. Add the cornstarch and vinegar and cook, stirring constantly, until the sauce has thickened.
4. Add the fructose, soy sauce, pineapple chunks and meat. Let the mixture stand for 1 hour.
5. Add the mushrooms, bell pepper, onion and water chestnuts. Cook until the vegetables are done, but still slightly crisp.
6. Serve over plain cooked white rice.

Makes 8 servings.

Each serving contains approximately:
  2 low-fat protein portions
  1 fruit portion
  ½ vegetable portion
  163 calories
  25 mg. cholesterol
  290 mg. sodium
½ cup cooked white rice contains approximately:
  1 starch portion

154

70 calories
0 mg. cholesterol
3 mg. sodium

Liver Teriyaki

1 cup soy sauce
1 tablespoon liquid fructose
3 garlic cloves, finely chopped
1½ teaspoons grated, peeled
   fresh gingerroot, or ¼
   teaspoon ground ginger
2 pounds calf's liver, sliced

1 tablespoon corn oil
4 onions, thinly sliced
2 cans (20 ounces each)
   crushed pineapple packed
   in natural juice, undrained
1 tablespoon cornstarch

1. Combine the soy sauce, fructose, garlic and gingerroot to make teriyaki marinade; mix well.
2. Marinate the sliced liver in the teriyaki mixture for several hours before cooking it.
3. Heat the corn oil in a large skillet. Add the sliced onions and sauté until completely tender and lightly browned.
4. Pour the juice from the cans of crushed pineapple into the skillet with the onions.
5. Combine ¼ cup of the teriyaki marinade with the cornstarch and mix until the cornstarch is thoroughly dissolved.
6. Add the cornstarch mixture to the onion mixture and bring to a boil. Reduce the heat and simmer, stirring constantly, until slightly thickened.
7. Remove from the heat and add the crushed pineapple and mix well.
8. Spoon half of the pineapple-onion mixture in a baking dish 8 x 12 inches. Remove the liver from the marinade and spread

Recipe continues . . .

155

evenly over the top of the pineapple-onion mixture. Do not overlap the slices.

9. Spoon the rest of the pineapple-onion mixture evenly over the top of the liver. Cover tightly with a lid or aluminum foil and bake in a preheated 350° oven for 15 minutes.

10. Remove from the oven and serve each slice of liver with the pineapple-onion mixture surrounding it. If you wish, you may serve remaining teriyaki marinade on the side to be used as a sauce.

Makes 8 servings.

Each serving contains approximately:
    3 medium-fat protein portions
    1¼ fruit portions
    1 vegetable portion
    322 calories
    388 mg. cholesterol
    2177 mg. sodium

Breads

You will find that many of the recipes in this section specifically list liquid fructose rather than simply fructose. The reason for this is that it is possible to reduce the amount of fat in the recipes when substituting liquid for granular fructose; therefore if you are using granular fructose you must increase the amount of fat in order for the recipes to work properly. By reducing the fats you also greatly reduce the number of calories per serving. It is for this reason that in some recipes I have used liquid fructose for baking.

Whole grain flours should not be sifted because the sifting process removes much of the bran from the flour, greatly reducing the amount of dietary fiber in the flour.

It is important to check the date on the package of yeast before using it. It is always a disappointment to find, after you have spent all of the time necessary to make bread dough and it does not rise, that the yeast was older than the prescribed limit for its effectiveness. It is for this reason that in each recipe containing yeast I mention checking the date on the package before using it.

Once you start baking your own breads, you will find that they are better than anything you can buy. If your time is limited, double your bread recipes and freeze one loaf to use at a future time.

As I mentioned in my introduction, using fructose shortens baking time and thus saves energy.

157

Canyon Ranch Bread

1¼ cups liquid nonfat milk
1 tablespoon fresh lemon juice
¼ cup finely chopped raisins
1 cup unprocessed wheat bran
¼ cup liquid fructose
1 tablespoon vanilla extract

1 egg, lightly beaten, or ¼ cup
  liquid egg substitute
1½ cups whole-wheat flour
1 tablespoon low-sodium baking powder

1. Combine the nonfat milk and lemon juice and mix well. Allow to stand for 5 minutes.
2. Combine the lemon-juice and milk mixture with the raisins, unprocessed wheat bran, liquid fructose and vanilla in a mixing bowl and mix well. Cover and allow to stand for 30 minutes.
3. Add the beaten egg or egg substitute to the bran mixture and mix well.
4. Combine the dry ingredients in another bowl and mix well. Add the liquid ingredients to the dry ingredients and mix thoroughly.
5. Spray a standard-sized loaf pan thoroughly with a nonstick spray. Place the dough in the pan and bake in a preheated 350° oven for 1 hour. Remove the bread from the oven and place the pan on its side on a rack to cool.
6. When the bread is cool enough to handle, remove it from the pan and cool it on the rack to room temperature. Wrap the cooled bread tightly in foil and refrigerate until cold before slicing.
7. To serve the bread, slice it lengthwise into halves. Slice each half into 12 pieces. Lightly spread each slice with corn oil margarine if desired. Again, wrap it tightly in aluminum foil and reheat in a preheated 325° oven for 30 minutes. This is a recipe I developed for the Canyon Ranch in Tucson, Arizona. It is a delicious, high-fiber, low-sodium, fat-free bread.

Makes 1 loaf (24 slices).

1 slice contains approximately:
    ¼ fruit portion
    ½ starch portion
    45 calories
    13 mg. cholesterol
    9.8 mg. sodium

Toasted Tortilla Triangles

12 corn tortillas
Salt

1. Cut each tortilla into 6 pie-shaped pieces.
2. Place half of the tortilla triangles on a cookie sheet, spread out, and salt lightly.
3. Bake in a 400° oven for 10 minutes.
4. Remove from the oven, turn each one over, and return them to the 400° oven for 3 more minutes.
5. Place second half of the tortilla triangles on a cookie sheet and repeat the process.

   If you prefer smaller chips, cut the tortillas into smaller triangles before toasting them. Sprinkle the tortillas with cumin-seed or chili powder for different flavors.

6 tortilla triangles contain:
    1 starch portion
    70 calories
    0 mg. cholesterol
    trace sodium without salt

Fat-Free Dill Bread

1 cake compressed yeast, or 1
   package active dry yeast
   (check the date on the
   package)
¼ cup warm water
1 cup low fat cottage cheese
4 teaspoons fructose

¼ cup minced onion
¼ teaspoon baking soda
1 egg, lightly beaten
2 tablespoons dill seed
1 teaspoon salt
2 cups all-purpose flour

1. Soften the yeast in ¼ cup warm water.
2. Warm the cottage cheese in a saucepan.
3. Add the yeast in the water to the warm cottage cheese.
4. Add the fructose, minced onion, baking soda, beaten egg, dill
seed and salt. Mix well.
5. Add the sifted flour, a little at a time, mixing well.
6. Cover and allow to stand at room temperature for several
hours, or until doubled in bulk.
7. Stir dough until again reduced to original size, and put in a
well-oiled, standard-sized metal loaf pan.
8. Cover the loaf pan and allow the dough again to double in
bulk.
9. Bake in a 350° oven for 40 minutes.
   This bread is delicious right from the oven. However, it's
much easier to slice when cool. Wrap sliced bread in foil and
store in the refrigerator until ready to use. Warm in the oven
before serving.

Makes 18 slices.

1 slice contains approximately:
   1 starch portion
   70 calories
   15 mg. cholesterol
   196 mg. sodium

160

Orange Rye Bread

1 package active dry yeast
(check the date on the
package)
¾ cup warm water
3 tablespoons liquid fructose
2 tablespoons grated orange
rind

1½ teaspoons fennel seed
1½ teaspoons caraway seed
1 cup rye flour
2 tablespoons corn oil margarine
1½ cups all-purpose flour
Additional flour for kneading

1. Combine the warm water and yeast and allow to stand 5 minutes, or until the yeast is completely dissolved.
2. Add the fructose, orange rind and fennel and caraway seeds to the yeast mixture in a large mixing bowl.
3. Slowly add the rye flour and corn oil margarine and mix well.
4. Add the all-purpose flour a little at a time. It will be necessary to knead the last of the flour into the dough. Continue kneading the bread until all ingredients are thoroughly mixed.
5. Place the dough back in the bowl. Cover the dough with a damp cloth and let it double in bulk.
6. Knead the dough again until it is smooth and elastic. Place it back in the bowl and allow again to double in bulk.
7. Knead the dough again, form it into an oval, and place it in a greased and floured loaf pan. Cover the pan with a cloth and again allow almost to double in bulk.
8. Bake in a preheated 375° oven for 35 minutes.

I often make this into 6 small loaves and serve each guest an individual loaf. One small loaf also makes a good hostess gift.

Makes 1 loaf (20 slices).

1 slice contains approximately:
1 starch portion
70 calories
0 mg. cholesterol
11 mg. sodium

Irish Soda Bread

2 cups all-purpose flour
2 teaspoons baking powder
½ teaspoon baking soda
½ teaspoon salt
2 tablespoons fructose
½ cup cold corn oil margarine

⅔ cup liquid nonfat milk
1 egg, lightly beaten
½ cup chopped raisins
2 teaspoons caraway seeds
Additional milk for glazing

1. Combine the flour, baking powder, baking soda, salt and fructose in a large mixing bowl and mix well.
2. Add the cold margarine and, using a pastry blender, blend the mixture until it has the consistency of coarse cornmeal.
3. Combine the milk and beaten egg and mix well. Add to the flour and margarine mixture and mix well. Add the chopped raisins and caraway seeds and mix thoroughly.
4. Remove the dough to a floured board and knead for 2 or 3 minutes.
5. Place the dough in a greased and floured 8-inch round pan and press down so that the dough fills the entire pan. Cut a deep crease on the top of the bread so that the sides will not crack while the bread is baking.
6. Brush the top lightly with milk. Bake in a preheated 375° oven for 35 to 40 minutes.

Makes 20 slices.

1 slice contains approximately:
    1 starch portion
    ½ fruit portion
    90 calories
    13 mg. cholesterol
    142 mg. sodium

Lettuce Bread

⅔ cup liquid fructose
¼ cup corn oil
1 egg, lightly beaten
1½ cups all-purpose flour
2 teaspoons baking powder
½ teaspoon baking soda
½ teaspoon salt

⅛ teaspoon ground mace
⅛ teaspoon ground ginger
1 teaspoon freshly grated
    lemon rind
1 cup finely shredded lettuce
¼ cup finely chopped walnuts

1. Combine the fructose, corn oil and egg and mix well. Set aside.
2. In another bowl, combine the flour, baking powder, baking soda, salt, mace and ginger and mix well.
3. Combine the wet ingredients with the dry ingredients and again mix well.
4. Add the lemon rind, lettuce and walnuts to the batter and mix well.
5. Pour the batter into a well-greased and floured loaf pan.
6. Bake in a 350° oven for 45 minutes, or until a knife inserted in the center of the loaf comes out clean and dry.

Makes 20 slices.

1 slice contains approximately:
    1 starch portion
    70 calories
    13 mg. cholesterol
    117 mg. sodium

163

Banana Bread

6 tablespoons corn oil margarine

2 cups all-purpose flour

⅛ teaspoon salt

1½ teaspoons baking soda

⅔ cup fructose

2 eggs, lightly beaten

½ cup buttermilk

1 teaspoon vanilla extract

3 ripe bananas, mashed with a fork

1. Allow the margarine to come to room temperature so that it is soft. Cream the margarine and 1 cup of the flour, mixed with the salt, baking soda and fructose.
2. Add the beaten eggs and mix well.
3. Add the remaining flour and buttermilk alternately.
4. Add the vanilla and mashed bananas.
5. Put the dough in a standard-size metal loaf pan which has been greased with part of the margarine (I use what is left on the wrapper) and floured lightly.
6. Bake at 350° for 1 hour and 15 minutes. Cool the bread on its side.
7. When cool, wrap the bread in aluminum foil or put it in a tight plastic bag in the refrigerator. If possible, keep it for 2 days before eating it.
8. To serve, slice the bread thinly, wrap tightly in foil, and put in a 300° oven for about 10 minutes, or until it is hot.

Makes 18 slices.

1 slice contains approximately:
    1 starch portion
    1 fat portion
    ¼ fruit portion
    125 calories
    28.2 mg. cholesterol
    178 mg. sodium

Show-off Popovers

4 egg whites, at room temperature
1 cup liquid nonfat milk
1 cup all-purpose flour

¼ teaspoon salt
¼ teaspoon fructose
2 tablespoons melted corn oil margarine

1. Preheat oven to 450°.
2. Put all ingredients in a blender container and blend at medium speed for 15 seconds. *Do not overmix!*
3. Pour the batter into five 3½-inch custard cups which have been well sprayed with a nonstick coating.
4. Bake in a 450° oven for 20 minutes. Reduce heat to 350° and bake for 20 more minutes.

These are about as showy as anything you can serve.

Makes 5 giant popovers.

1 popover contains approximately:
    1 fat portion
    1 starch portion
    125 calories
    .4 mg. cholesterol
    88 mg. sodium

VARIATION: *Cinnamon Popovers: Add ½ teaspoon ground cinnamon.*

Lavash

2 cups unbleached white flour
1 teaspoon salt
1 package active dry yeast (check the date on the package)

2 tablespoons corn oil margarine, melted
½ teaspoon fructose
⅔ cup warm water
2 tablespoons sesame seeds

1. Combine the flour, salt and yeast in a large mixing bowl.
2. Combine the melted margarine, fructose and warm water and mix well.
3. Slowly add the liquid mixture to the dry ingredients, stirring constantly.
4. Knead the dough until it is smooth and elastic. Rub corn oil margarine over the entire surface of the dough ball.
5. Place the dough back in the bowl and cover the bowl with a plastic wrap or aluminum foil. Place a hot damp towel over the covered bowl and allow to rise until doubled in bulk, 1 to 2 hours.
6. Preheat the oven to 400°. Divide the dough into 2 pieces. Place ½ tablespoon of the sesame seeds on a cookie sheet.
7. Place one of the dough balls on the cookie sheet and press it out as thin as possible. Turn it over and put another ½ tablespoon of the sesame seeds on the cookie sheet. Using a rolling pin, roll the dough out as thin as possible without tearing it. Allow to rest for 5 minutes.
8. Bake the *lavash* on the lowest rack in the oven until it is light golden brown with darker highlights on it, about 15 minutes. While the *lavash* is cooking, repeat the process exactly with the second ball of dough, using a second cookie sheet.

To serve, break *lavash* into pieces. Many elegant restaurants have baskets of *lavash* on the table routinely for cocktails

166

as well as for a bread to eat with meals. *Lavash* will keep for a long time if wrapped tightly and stored in a dry place.

Makes about 30 *lavash* crackers.

1 piece contains approximately:
   ¾ starch portion
   52 calories
   0 mg. cholesterol
   81 mg. sodium

Pancakes

2 eggs
¼ teaspoon baking soda
¼ teaspoon salt
1 teaspoon fructose

2½ teaspoons baking powder
1 cup buttermilk
1 cup all-purpose flour
1 teaspoon corn oil margarine

1. Beat the eggs, baking soda, salt, fructose and baking powder together until frothy.
2. Add the buttermilk and flour. Mix well.
3. Heat a pan that has nonstick coating.
4. Add the margarine and allow it to melt as the pan heats. When the pan is hot, wipe out the margarine with a paper towel.
5. Use a soup ladle to pour out the batter and cook the pancakes over moderate heat.

Makes twenty 3-inch pancakes.

2 pancakes contain approximately:
   1 starch portion
   70 calories
   52 mg. cholesterol
   87 mg. sodium

Pineapple Muffins

2 cups all-purpose flour
4 teaspoons baking powder
⅛ teaspoon salt
¼ cup liquid fructose
1 egg

1½ teaspoons vanilla extract
2 tablespoons corn oil
1 can (20 ounces) unsweetened crushed pineapple,
undrained

1. Preheat the oven to 425°.
2. Put the flour in a large bowl. Add the baking powder and salt and mix thoroughly.
3. In another bowl, combine the liquid fructose, egg, vanilla and corn oil and beat lightly with a fork or a wire whisk.
4. Add the crushed pineapple and all of the juice from the can to the egg mixture and mix thoroughly.
5. Pour the wet ingredients into the bowl of dry ingredients and stir until well mixed, being careful not to overmix the muffin batter.
6. Spoon batter into sixteen 2½-inch muffin tins (⅔ full). Bake at 425° for 25 minutes.

Makes 16 muffins.

1 muffin contains approximately:
    1 starch portion
    ¾ fruit portion
    100 calories
    16 mg. cholesterol
    83 mg. sodium

Crêpes

1 cup liquid nonfat milk
¾ cup all-purpose flour
¼ teaspoon fructose
¼ teaspoon salt

½ cup liquid egg substitute
1 teaspoon melted corn oil
   margarine

1. Put milk, flour, fructose and salt in a bowl and beat with an egg beater until well mixed.
2. Beat in the egg substitute and mix well.
3. In an omelet or crêpe pan with nonstick coating, melt 1 teaspoon corn oil margarine. When the margarine is melted and the pan is hot, tilt the pan to make sure the entire pan is coated. Pour the melted margarine into the crêpe batter and mix well.
4. Pour in just enough crêpe batter to barely cover the bottom of the pan, about 2 tablespoons, and tilt the pan from side to side to spread the batter evenly.
5. When the edges start to curl, carefully turn the crêpe with a spatula and brown the other side.
6. To keep the crêpes pliable, put them in a covered casserole in a warm oven as you make them.

TO FREEZE: *Put a piece of aluminum foil or wax paper between crêpes and wrap them well so that they are not exposed to the air. Before using, bring to room temperature and put them in a 300° oven for 20 minutes so they are soft and pliable. Otherwise they will break when you try to fold them.*

Makes 12 crêpes.

1 crêpe contains approximately:
   ½ starch portion
   35 calories
   2 mg. cholesterol
   81 mg. sodium

169

Popular Porridge

(A ready-to-eat breakfast treat)

1½ cups old-fashioned rolled
    oats
¼ cup chopped raw almonds
½ cup chopped raisins

1 teaspoon ground cinnamon
2 cups water
1 tablespoon liquid fructose

1. Combine all ingredients except the water and fructose in a mixing bowl and mix well.
2. Combine the water and fructose and mix well. Combine the liquid ingredients with the dry ingredients and again mix thoroughly.
3. Cover and refrigerate for 2 days before serving.

    I call this Popular Porridge because once you have made it you will want this ready-to-eat breakfast treat in your refrigerator all of the time. It is delicious served with plain low-fat yogurt or nonfat milk. I also like it with low-fat cottage cheese and occasionally even serve it for dessert.

Makes 4 cups.

½ cup contains approximately:
    1 starch portion
    1 fruit portion
    110 calories
    0 mg. cholesterol
    trace sodium

Date Nut Waffles

1 cup liquid nonfat milk, lukewarm
1 package active dry yeast
(check the date on the package)
3 eggs, beaten
2 tablespoons corn oil

2 tablespoons liquid fructose
2 teaspoons vanilla extract
2 cups whole-wheat flour
¼ teaspoon salt
1 teaspoon ground cinnamon
½ cup finely chopped dates
¼ cup finely chopped walnuts

1. Combine the warm milk and yeast and mix well.
2. Combine the eggs with the oil, liquid fructose and vanilla. Mix
well and add to the yeast mixture.
3. Combine the flour, salt and cinnamon and mix into liquid
mixture, a little at a time, blending well.
4. Cover the bowl with a cloth and allow to rise in a warm place
for about 1 hour.
5. Add the dates and walnuts and mix well.
6. Baked in a hot oiled waffle iron or iron with nonstick coating.

Makes 8 waffles.

1 waffle contains approximately:
  2 starch portions
  1 fat portion
  1 fruit portion
  225 calories
  95 mg. cholesterol
  108 mg. sodium

Fettuccine Pasta

2 cups semolina flour or all-purpose flour
1 teaspoon fructose
1½ tablespoons corn oil
¾ cup warm water

1. Using a pastry blender, combine the flour and oil, cutting through it evenly until well mixed.
2. Add water, a little at a time, to form a firm ball of dough. This process is best done by kneading by hand until the dough becomes shiny, smooth and elastic.
3. Cover the ball with an inverted bowl and allow to stand at room temperature for at least 1 hour. Then divide the ball of dough into 4 equal parts.
4. Flatten each part with the palm of your hand into a square-shaped piece about 1 inch thick.
5. With a heavy rolling pin, roll out each part of dough lengthwise; turn, and roll out crosswise. Continue with this until you have a sheet of the desired thickness, about ⅛ inch thick or less. Do this with each separate piece of dough. (To prevent sticking while rolling out the dough, carefully lift it and sprinkle a little more flour on the board.)
6. To cut fettuccine, simply roll the thin pasta into jelly-roll shape. Cut this into ¼-inch slices and *quickly* unroll into strips to prevent sticking together.

TO COOK PASTA: *Use an 8-quart kettle filled with water, adding 2 tablespoons of salt and 1 tablespoon of corn oil. Bring the water to a boil and add the pasta. Boil for approximately 5 minutes, or to taste. Pasta should be what the Italians call "al dente," meaning it has a slight resilience when eaten. Pasta made with semolina flour will take a couple of minutes longer to cook. Pour the* *water and pasta into a colander and drain well. The fettuccine are now ready to be mixed with your favorite sauce.*

Makes 4 cups cooked pasta.

½ cup cooked pasta contains approximately:
    1 starch portion
    68 calories
    0 mg. cholesterol
    trace sodium

Desserts and
Dessert Sauces

Most people do not think of desserts as being part of a weight maintenance program; however, it is possible to create dramatic desserts which are spectacular to serve and delicious to eat, *and low in calories* as well.

Surprise your friends with a Cold Banana Soufflé topped with a little Caribbean Rum Sauce the next time you entertain; but day in and day out get in the habit of serving the fresh fruits available during the year. When fruits are not quite ripe, sprinkle a little fructose on them or spread a little liquid fructose over the top of each serving and allow it to stand for several minutes. The fructose will heighten the natural fruit flavor and make the fruit seem to be more ripe than it is. Many people who have always used salt on melons find that a little fructose is an even greater flavor heightener for melon than salt.

Fun 'n Fancy Cookies

(With overnight possibilities)

6 tablespoons corn oil marga-
    rine, at room temperature
½ cup liquid fructose
1 egg, lightly beaten, or ¼ cup
    liquid egg substitute

1 teaspoon vanilla extract
2 cups all-purpose flour
¼ teaspoon salt
2 teaspoons baking powder

1. Combine the margarine and liquid fructose and mix, using a wire whisk or a pastry blender, until completely smooth.
2. Add the beaten egg and vanilla. Again beat well.
3. Combine the flour, salt and baking powder and mix well.
4. Stir the dry ingredients into the liquid ingredients and mix thoroughly.
5. After mixing the dough, you may either bake drop cookies immediately, or form the dough into a 2-inch-diameter roll on a piece of foil, wrap dough in the foil, and put in the refrigerator for at least 12 hours or overnight.
6. To make drop cookies, drop on a cookie sheet by teaspoons and bake in a preheated 400° oven for 8 to 10 minutes. The advantage of refrigerator cookies is that they may be rolled out and cut into decorative shapes before baking, or you may roll the entire roll of cookies in nutmeats and then slice thinly, making a border around each cookie, or you may simply slice the roll thinly and sprinkle a little fructose on the top of the cookies while they are still warm to make "sugar cookies." The refrigerated cookie dough is also baked in a preheated 400° oven for 8 to 10 minutes.

Makes 6 dozen cookies.

2 cookies contain approximately:

½ starch portion	56 calories
¼ fat portion	7 mg. cholesterol
¼ fruit portion	48 mg. sodium

175

Jazzy Jelled Water

(The perfect dessert—delicious but not disastrous)

1 envelope unflavored gelatin
¼ cup cold water
¾ cup boiling water
2 tablespoons liquid fructose
¼ teaspoon vanilla extract

1 teaspoon of your favorite-flavored extract (or instant coffee, etc.)
1 cup cold water

1. Put the gelatin and cold water in a cup and let the gelatin soften.
2. Add the boiling water and stir until the gelatin is completely dissolved.
3. Add the fructose and extracts, and place in the refrigerator until firm.
4. When the mixture is firm, put into a blender container, add the cup of cold water, and blend until frothy.
5. Pour into sherbet glasses and garnish with mint sprigs.

Makes 6 servings.

Each serving contains approximately:
   ¼ fruit portion
   10 calories
   0 mg. cholesterol
   trace sodium

Rhubarb Compote

2 pounds rhubarb, cut into 1-inch pieces (4 cups)
2 teaspoons ground cinnamon
1 tablespoon grated orange rind
¾ cup fructose

1 envelope unflavored gelatin
2 tablespoons water
¼ cup boiling water
1 orange, peeled and sliced for garnish

176

1. Preheat the oven to 350°.
2. Combine the rhubarb, cinnamon, grated orange rind and fructose in a casserole and mix well.
3. Cover and bake for 40 minutes. Cool to room temperature.
4. Soften the gelatin in the 2 tablespoons of water. Add the boiling water and stir until the gelatin is completely dissolved.
5. Pour the dissolved gelatin mixture into the baked rhubarb and mix well.
6. Garnish with orange slices.
7. Refrigerate until firm before serving.

Makes 8 servings.

Each serving contains approximately:
> 1 fruit portion
> 1 vegetable portion
> 65 calories
> 1 mg. cholesterol
> trace sodium

VARIATION: *Rhubarb compote may also be used as a pie filling.*

Strawberries Hoffmann-La Roche

1 cup liquid nonfat milk
1 tablespoon cornstarch
2 tablespoon fructose
1½ teaspoons vanilla extract
2 tablespoons Grand Marnier
2 egg whites, at room temperature

⅛ teaspoon cream of tartar
4 cups sliced fresh strawberries
8 whole strawberries

Recipe continues . . .

177

1. Pour the milk into a saucepan. Add the cornstarch and fructose and stir until the cornstarch is thoroughly dissolved.
2. Place the pan on low heat and bring to a boil. Simmer, stirring constantly with a wire whisk, until slightly thickened.
Remove the pan from the heat and cool to room temperature.
4. Add the vanilla extract and Grand Marnier to the cooled sauce and mix well.
5. Combine the egg whites and cream of tartar and beat until stiff but not dry.
6. Fold the beaten egg whites into the sauce. Combine the sauce and the sliced strawberries. Mix well.
7. Divide evenly into 8 sherbet glasses. Place a whole strawberry on top of each serving for garnish.

I created this recipe for dessert for a dinner party given by Hoffman-La Roche, Inc., at Joseph's Restaurant in Boston. I liked it so much that I asked their permission to include it in this book. It is not only delicious and beautiful, it is also very low in sodium.

Makes 8 servings.

Each serving contains approximately:
  1 starch portion
  70 calories
  trace cholesterol
  15 mg. sodium

Raspberry Mousse

2 envelopes unflavored gelatin
¼ cup cool water
¼ cup boiling water
3 cups fresh or unsweetened
  frozen raspberries

1 can (8 ounces) unsweetened
  crushed pineapple, undrained
1 teaspoon vanilla extract
2 tablespoons liquid fructose
½ cup sour cream

Sauce:
>½ cup sour cream
>1½ teaspoons liquid fructose
>½ teaspoon vanilla extract
>Fresh mint sprigs for garnish (optional)

1. Soften the gelatin in the cool water for 5 minutes.
2. Add the boiling water to the softened gelatin and stir until the gelatin is completely dissolved.
3. Put 2 cups of the raspberries in a blender container. Set the remaining cup of raspberries aside to add later.
4. Add the dissolved gelatin mixture to the raspberries in the blender container; then add the crushed pineapple and all of the juice from the can, the vanilla extract, fructose and sour cream. Blend until smooth.
5. Pour the mixture into a bowl and add the remaining raspberries. Mix well.
6. Spoon the mixture into 6 small soufflé dishes or 1 large dessert dish. Refrigerate until firm before serving. It looks especially nice in a decorative mold.
7. Before serving, make the sauce. Combine the remaining ½ cup of sour cream, the fructose and vanilla extract and mix with a wire whisk.
8. Spoon some sauce over the top of each serving of Raspberry Mousse. Garnish each serving with a sprig of fresh mint if available.

Makes 6 servings.

Each serving contains approximately:
>1¾ fruit portions
>1¼ fat portions
>126 calories
>21 mg. cholesterol
>19 mg. sodium

Dutch Rum Soufflé

2 envelopes unflavored gelatin
1 cup cold water
½ cup carob powder
½ cup liquid fructose
1½ teaspoons dry instant coffee
1 tablespoon vanilla extract
1½ teaspoons rum extract

2 egg yolks, or ½ cup liquid egg substitute
8 egg whites
⅛ teaspoon cream of tartar
1 cup canned evaporated skimmed milk, cold

1. Fold a sheet of wax paper in half lengthwise and wrap around the rim of a 7½-inch (1½-quart) soufflé dish to form a wax-paper collar that extends at least 3 inches above the rim of the dish. Secure the collar with tape.

2. Empty both envelopes of gelatin into the cup of cold water and allow to soften for 5 minutes.

3. Combine the carob powder, liquid fructose, dry instant coffee, and vanilla and rum extracts and mix thoroughly. Set aside.

4. Put the egg yolks or liquid egg substitute in the top portion of a double boiler and beat until foamy.

5. Add the softened gelatin to the egg yolks or liquid egg substitute and mix well. Place over simmering water and cook, stirring constantly, until thick enough to coat a metal spoon. *Do not allow the mixture to come to a boil!*

6. Remove the pan from the heat and add the carob mixture. Mix well and place in the refrigerator until thickened slightly, about 45 minutes.

7. Combine the egg whites and cream of tartar in a large, clean non-plastic bowl and beat, using an electric mixer, until stiff but not dry; set aside.

8. In another bowl, beat the cup of cold, canned evaporated skimmed milk until it has doubled in volume. (Plain nonfat milk

180

will not work in this recipe. It must be canned evaporated skimmed milk, and it must be cold.

9. Combine the whipped milk with the mixture from the refrigerator and mix thoroughly.

10. Fold the beaten egg whites gently into the mixture and fold until no streaks of white show.

11. Pour the soufflé mixture into the collared soufflé dish. Refrigerate for at least 4 hours before removing the collar and serving.

Makes 16 servings.

Each serving contains approximately:
  1 fruit portion
  40 calories
  32 mg. cholesterol
  46 mg. sodium

Crêpes Suzette

1 cup fresh orange juice
2 teaspoons cornstarch
2 tablespoons liquid fructose
1 tablespoon freshly grated orange rind (use only the colored part of the orange peel)
¼ cup orange liqueur (Grand Marnier is best)

1 tablespoon corn oil margarine
12 Crêpes (see index)
1 tablespoon powdered or granular fructose
2 tablespoons brandy (optional)

Recipe continues . . .

181

1. Pour the orange juice into a saucepan. Add the cornstarch and fructose to the juice, and stir until the cornstarch is dissolved.
2. Bring slowly to a boil and simmer, stirring constantly with a wire whisk, until slightly thickened. Remove the pan from the heat.
3. Add the grated orange rind, orange liqueur and corn oil margarine. Stir until the margarine is completely melted. Pour the sauce into a heated chafing dish.
4. Dip both sides of each crêpe into the sauce. Fold the crêpe in half and then in half again, forming a triangle, and put it on a plate or serving platter.
5. Continue until all the crêpes have been dipped and folded and arranged on the serving dish.
6. Sprinkle the powdered fructose evenly over the crêpes. At this point you may add the brandy to the sauce remaining in the chafing dish and ignite it with a lighted match. Shake the chafing dish gently back and forth while spooning the flaming liquid over the folded crêpes until the flame goes out. Be careful; don't burn yourself!

Makes 6 servings.

Each serving contains approximately:
    1 starch portion
    1 fruit portion
    1 fat portion
    153 calories
    0 mg. cholesterol
    180 mg. sodium

Basic White Cake

1½ cups pastry or cake flour
2 teaspoons baking powder
¼ teaspoon salt
⅛ teaspoon cream of tartar
3 egg whites, at room temperature

½ cup corn oil margarine
⅔ cup fructose
1 teaspoon vanilla extract
½ cup liquid nonfat milk

1. Preheat the oven to 350°.
2. Grease the sides of a 9-inch cake pan. Cut wax paper to fit the bottom of the pan. (If you use a cake pan with nonstick coating it is not necessary to grease the sides, but still put wax paper in the bottom.)
3. Sift together the flour, baking powder and salt and set aside.
4. Add the cream of tartar to the egg whites. Beat the egg whites until they hold soft peaks and set aside.
5. Using the same beater, in a large mixing bowl cream the corn oil margarine, fructose and vanilla extract together until light and fluffy.
6. Add the sifted flour and milk alternately to the margarine-fructose mixture until the batter is throughly mixed.
7. Fold the beaten egg whites into the batter, being careful not to overmix.
8. Spread the batter evenly in the cake pan and bake in the 350° oven for 25 minutes. Cool on a rack.

Makes 16 servings.

Each serving contains approximately:
1½ starch portions
1 fruit portion
145 calories
trace cholesterol
131 mg. sodium

183

Cold Banana Soufflé

2 envelopes unflavored gelatin
1 cup cold water
2 egg yolks or ½ cup liquid egg
  substitute
3 small bananas, puréed (1 cup
  puréed banana)
1 tablespoon vanilla extract

8 egg whites
⅓ cup fructose
1 cup canned evaporated
  skimmed milk, cold
2 cups Caribbean Rum Sauce
  (see index)

1. Fold a sheet of wax paper in half lengthwise and wrap around
the rim of a 7½-inch (1½-quart) soufflé dish to form a wax-paper
collar which extends at least 3 inches above the rim of the dish.
Secure the collar with tape.
2. Empty both envelopes of gelatin into the cup of cold water and
allow to soften for 5 minutes.
3. Put the egg yolks or liquid egg substitute in the top portion of
a double boiler and beat until foamy.
4. Add the softened gelatin to the egg yolks or liquid egg substitute and mix well. Place over simmering water and cook, stirring
constantly, until thick enough to coat a metal spoon. *Do not allow
the mixture to come to a boil!*
5. Remove the pan from the heat and add the puréed banana
and vanilla extract. Mix well and place in the refrigerator until
slightly thickened, about 20 minutes.
6. Put the egg whites in a large, clean non-plastic bowl and beat,
using an electric mixer, until frothy.
7. Slowly add ⅓ cup of fructose and continue to beat the egg
whites until stiff but not dry, set aside.
8. In another bowl, beat the cup of cold, canned evaporated
skimmed milk until it has doubled in volume. (Plain nonfat milk
will not work in this recipe. It must be canned evaporated
skimmed milk and it must be cold.)

9. Combine the whipped milk with the mixture from the refrigerator and mix thoroughly.

10. Fold the beaten egg white and fructose mixture gently into the other ingredients, folding until no streaks of white show.

11. Pour the soufflé into the collared soufflé dish and refrigerate for at least 4 hours before removing the collar and serving.

When serving this gorgeous, awe-inspiring cold soufflé to your guests, spoon 2 tablespoons of Caribbean Rum Sauce over the top of each serving.

Makes 16 servings.

Each serving contains approximately:
1 fruit portion
½ fat portion
63 calories
.2 mg. cholesterol
59 mg. sodium

Jelled Milk

1 envelope unflavored gelatin
2 tablespoons cold water
¼ cup boiling water
1 cup liquid nonfat milk

1. Soften the gelatin in 2 tablespoons of cold water in a bowl.

2. Add ¼ cup of boiling water and mix until the gelatin is thoroughly dissolved.

Recipe continues . . .

185

3. Add the milk and mix well.

4. Cover and refrigerate. When mixture is jelled, it is ready to use in many low-calorie recipes, especially desserts.

Makes 1 cup.

1 cup contains approximately:
 1 nonfat milk portion
 80 calories
 2.3 mg. cholesterol
 127 mg. sodium

English Trifle

¼ cup finely chopped raw almonds
1 Basic White Cake (see index), or 1 box fructose-sweetened white cake mix prepared according to directions on box (see Appendix 4)
1 cup Strawberry Jam (see index), or commercial fructose-sweetened jam (see Appendix 4)

1½ cups liquid nonfat milk
2 eggs, lightly beaten, or ½ cup liquid egg substitute
3 tablespoons fructose
1 teaspoon vanilla extract
¼ cup sherry
2 cups fresh peaches, or frozen or canned peaches without added sugar

1. Preheat the oven to 350°. Place the almonds in the oven for 8 to 10 minutes or until golden brown. Watch them carefully as they burn easily. Set aside.

2. Spread the baked white cake with the strawberry jam, cut into 1-inch cubes, and set aside.

3. Bring the milk to the boiling point in the top part of a double

186

boiler. Slowly add the beaten eggs or egg substitute, beating with a wire whisk.

4. Continue cooking until the mixture coats a metal spoon. Remove from the heat and cool to room temperature.

5. When custard is cool, add the fructose, vanilla and sherry and mix thoroughly.

6. Place half of the cubed cake in the bottom of a large bowl. Put 1 cup of the sliced peaches on top of the cake. Pour half of the custard sauce over the top of the peaches.

7. Repeat with the remaining cake, peaches and sauce. Sprinkle the toasted almonds evenly over the top.

8. Cover and refrigerate for several hours before serving. Remove from the refrigerator for at least 1 hour before serving. Trifle has a better flavor if cool but not really cold.

Makes 12 servings.

Each serving contains approximately:
 2 starch portions
 1 fat portion
 ¼ medium-fat protein portion
 1½ fruit portions
 264 calories
 42 mg. cholesterol
 201 mg. sodium

Hawaiian Carrot Cake

1 cup whole-wheat flour
1 teaspoon baking powder
¾ teaspoon baking soda
¼ teaspoon salt
1 teaspoon ground cinnamon
¼ cup corn oil
¼ cup liquid fructose

2 eggs, lightly beaten, or ⅓ cup
    liquid egg substitute
1 can (20 ounces) pineapple
    chunks packed in juice,
    drained
1 cup grated raw carrots
¼ cup chopped walnuts

1. Preheat the oven to 350°. Lightly grease the sides of an 8½-inch-square cake pan. Cut wax paper to fit the bottom of the pan. (If using a pan with nonstick coating, put wax paper on the bottom but it is not necessary to grease the sides.)
2. Combine the flour, baking powder, baking soda, salt and cinnamon in a large mixing bowl.
3. In another bowl, combine the oil, fructose and eggs and mix well.
4. Add the liquid ingredients to the dry ingredients and again mix well.
5. Put the pineapple chunks in a blender and blend just enough to chop the pineapple coarsely, or chop the pineapple with a knife. Add the chopped pineapple to the cake batter.
6. Add the grated carrots and the chopped walnuts and mix well.
7. Pour the batter into the cake pan and bake at 350° for approximately 35 minutes.
8. Cool to room temperature and cover so the cake will not get dry. If not serving immediately, store in the refrigerator.

Makes 16 servings.

Each serving contains approximately:
1 starch portion	154 calories
1 fruit portion	32 mg. cholesterol
¾ fat portion	121 mg. sodium

188

Perfect Piecrust

1 cup all-purpose flour
¼ teaspoon salt
¼ cup corn oil
3 tablespoons ice water

1. Preheat the oven to 375°.
2. Put the flour and salt in a 9-inch pie pan and mix well.
3. Measure the oil in a large measuring cup. Add the water to the oil and mix well, using a fork.
4. Slowly add the liquid to the flour mixture in the pie pan, mixing it with the same fork. Continue mixing until all ingredients are well blended.
5. Press into shape with your fingers. Make sure that the crust covers the entire inner surface of the pie pan evenly.
6. Prick the bottom of the crust with a fork in several places. Bake in the 375° oven for 20 to 25 minutes, or until golden brown, if the recipe calls for a prebaked piecrust.

    I used to hate making my own piecrust because I always messed up the entire kitchen and had flour all over me and the floor. Then one day when I was in a hurry I just put all of the ingredients in the pie pan, carefully mixed them together and then pressed the dough out with my fingers. It was so delicious and so easy that I have never gone back to rolling out dough on a floured board again. This recipe has actually made pie making fun for me. That is why it's called Perfect Piecrust.

Makes one 9-inch piecrust.

1 piecrust contains approximately:
    6½ starch portions
    12 fat portions
    995 calories
    0 mg. cholesterol
    550 mg. sodium

South Seas Pineapple Pie

1 Graham-Cracker Piecrust
  (see index) baked
1 envelope unflavored gelatin
2 tablespoons cool water
¼ cup boiling water
¾ cup low-fat cottage cheese
¼ cup liquid nonfat milk

1 teaspoon vanilla extract
4 teaspoons fructose
1 can (20 ounces) crushed
  pineapple, packed in natural
  juice, undrained
Ground cinnamon for
  garnish

1. Soften the gelatin in the 2 tablespoons of cool water.
2. Add the boiling water and stir until the gelatin is completely dissolved.
3. Put the gelatin mixture in a blender container with all other ingredients except the pineapple and blend thoroughly.
4. Pour the mixture into a bowl. Add the entire can of crushed pineapple, including the juice from the can, and mix well.
5. Pour the mixture into the baked piecrust and sprinkle with cinnamon.
6. Refrigerate until firm before serving.

Makes 10 servings.

Each serving contains approximately:
  ½ fruit portion
  1 starch portion
  ¼ low-fat protein portion
  ¼ fat portion
  145 calories
  .9 mg. cholesterol
  156 mg. sodium

VARIATION: *To save time, replace the Graham-Cracker Piecrust with a butter cookie crust made with a commercial Butter Cookie Mix (see Appendix 4):*

1 package Butter Cookie Mix (6¼ ounces)
1½ tablespoons corn oil

1. Combine the dry cookie mix and corn oil in a mixing bowl.
2. Using a fork or pastry blender, mix thoroughly. The dough will have the consistency of coarse cornmeal.
3. Place the dough in a 9-inch pie pan and press it into shape with your fingers, making sure it covers the entire inner surface of the pie pan.
4. Place the piecrust in a preheated 350° oven and bake for 10 to 15 minutes, or until pale golden brown.
5. Remove from the oven and cool to room temperature before filling.

Makes 10 servings of pie.

Each serving with Butter Cookie Crust contains approximately:
   1 fruit portion
   1 starch portion
   ¼ low-fat protein portion
   ¼ fat portion
   145 calories
   1.2 mg. cholesterol
   145 mg. sodium

Peanut Butter Pie

1 Graham-Cracker Piecrust (see index) baked
1 envelope unflavored gelatin
2 tablespoons cool water
¼ cup boiling water
1½ cups liquid nonfat milk

½ cup unhomogenized un-salted peanut butter
3 tablespoons liquid fructose
1½ teaspoons vanilla extract
Ground cinnamon for garnish

Recipe continues . . .

191

1. Soften the gelatin in 2 tablespoons of cool water.
2. Add the boiling water and stir until the gelatin is completely dissolved.
3. Combine all ingredients except the cinnamon in a blender container and blend until smooth and frothy.
4. Pour the liquid mixture into the baked pie shell. Sprinkle the top lightly with cinnamon for garnish.
5. Refrigerate until firm before serving.

Makes 10 servings.

Each serving contains approximately:
    ½ fruit portion
    1 starch portion
    ½ high-fat protein portion
    ½ fat portion
    183 calories
    .3 mg. cholesterol
    105 mg. sodium

Creamy Cheese Pie

Pie:
2 teaspoons corn oil margarine
4 graham-cracker squares, crushed
2 cups low-fat cottage cheese
¼ cup liquid fructose
2 teaspoons vanilla extract
1 teaspoon freshly grated lemon rind
1 teaspoon lemon juice

Topping:
1 cup sour cream
2 tablespoons liquid fructose
1½ teaspoons vanilla extract

1. Preheat the oven to 375°. Rub the 2 teaspoons of margarine evenly over the entire inner surface of a 9-inch pie plate.
2. Put the 4 graham-cracker squares in a plastic bag and roll them with a rolling pin until they are fine crumbs.
3. Sprinkle the crumbs evenly over the greased pie plate, pressing them down with your fingers to make certain they stick to the surface.
4. Put the cottage cheese and all other *pie* ingredients in a blender container and blend until completely smooth.
5. Pour the cottage cheese mixture into the crumb-lined plate and spread it out evenly.
6. Place pie in the center of the 375° oven and cook for 15 minutes.
7. While the pie is cooking, combine the topping ingredients in a mixing bowl and mix throughly.
8. Remove the pie from the oven and spread the topping evenly over the top. Return the pie to the 375° oven and continue cooking for 10 more minutes.
9. Remove the pie from the oven and cool on a rack to room temperature. Refrigerate until cold before serving. Just before serving the pie, rub the outside of the pie plate with a warm damp towel. This softens the margarine in the crust, making it less likely to stick to the bottom of the pie plate.

Makes 16 servings.

Each serving contains approximately:
    1 low-fat protein portion
    ½ fruit portion
    ½ fat portion
    98 calories
    9.3 mg. cholesterol
    138 mg. sodium

Graham-Cracker Piecrust

14 graham-cracker squares (1 cup crumbs)
2 tablespoons corn oil margarine, at room temperature
1 tablespoon liquid fructose

1. Put the graham crackers in a large plastic bag and roll them with a rolling pin until they are in fine crumbs. You may also use a food processor to make the crumbs.
2. Combine the graham-cracker crumbs, margarine and liquid fructose and mix thoroughly.
3. Place the crumb mixture in an 9-inch pie plate. Spread the mixture evenly over the entire inner surface of the pie plate with your fingers.
4. To bake, place the piecrust in a preheated 350° oven for 10 to 12 minutes. Cool the piecrust to room temperature before filling.

Makes one 9-inch piecrust (10 servings).

Each serving contains approximately:
    ¾ starch portion
    ½ fat portion
    76 calories
    .1 mg. cholesterol
    83 mg. sodium

Spiced Almonds

¼ cup fructose
¼ cup cornstarch
2 teaspoons ground cinnamon
½ teaspoon ground allspice
¼ teaspoon ground nutmeg

⅛ teaspoon ground ginger
1 egg white, lightly beaten
2 cups raw whole almonds (½ pound)

1. Preheat the oven to 250°.
2. Sift together the fructose, cornstarch, cinnamon, allspice, nutmeg and ginger into a bowl. Mix well and set aside.
3. Beat the egg white in a bowl. Add the almonds and mix well.
4. Coat each almond with the fructose-spice mixture. Shake excess dry mixture from each almond and place them on a well-oiled cookie sheet or one with nonstick coating. Be sure the almonds are well separated on the cookie sheet.
5. Bake in the 250° oven for 1½ hours. Remove the spiced almonds from the cookie sheet and store in a tightly covered container.

Makes 2 cups spiced almonds.

7 almonds contain approximately:
    1 fat portion
    ¼ fruit portion
    55 calories
    0 mg. cholesterol
    2.3 mg. sodium

Strawberry Jam

3 cups fresh strawberries or frozen strawberries without sugar
1½ teaspoons unflavored gelatin
1½ teaspoons lemon juice
2 teaspoons fructose

1. Put the strawberries in a covered saucepan. Cook, covered, over very low heat without water for about 10 minutes.
2. Remove the lid and bring the juice to the boiling point. Boil for 1 minute and remove from the heat.
3. Soften the gelatin in the lemon juice.
4. Pour some of the hot juice from the strawberries into the gelatin, and stir until the gelatin is completely dissolved.
5. Add the dissolved gelatin to the strawberries. Allow to cool to room temperature.
6. Add fructose and refrigerate.

Makes 3 cups.

1 cup contains approximately:
    1½ fruit portions
    60 calories
    0 mg. cholesterol
    1 mg. sodium

Whipped "Cream"

⅓ cup dry nonfat milk
⅓ cup ice water
2 teaspoons fresh lemon juice

1. Combine all ingredients and beat, using an electric mixer, until of the consistency of whipped cream. This will take between 5 and 10 minutes so do not be discouraged or think it will not work. This whipped "cream" should be used immediately or it will quickly return to its liquid state. If this happens, all is not lost; just refrigerate and beat again before using.

Makes 1¼ cups whipped "cream."

2 tablespoons contain approximately:
    ¼ nonfat milk portion
    20 calories
    .5 mg. cholesterol
    48 mg. sodium

VARIATION: *Sweet Whipped "Cream": Add 1 tablespoon of fructose and 1 teaspoon vanilla extract.*

2 tablespoons contain approximately:
    ¼ nonfat milk portion
    ¼ fruit portion
    30 calories
    .5 mg. cholesterol
    48 mg. sodium

"Amaretto" Sauce

½ cup Jelled Milk (see index)
½ cup liquid nonfat milk, cold
1 teaspoon vanilla extract
½ teaspoon almond extract
1 tablespoon fructose

1. Put all ingredients in a blender container and blend until smooth.
2. Allow to stand for a few minutes to thicken before spooning over fresh fruit or other desserts.
   I like "Amaretto" Sauce best on fresh peaches.

Makes 1 cup sauce.

2 tablespoons contain approximately:
   Free food, calories negligible
   .2 mg. cholesterol
   16 mg. sodium

"Coconut" Sauce

½ cup Jelled Milk (See index)
½ cup liquid nonfat milk, cold
½ teaspoon vanilla extract
½ teaspoon coconut extract
1 tablespoon fructose

198

1. Put all ingredients in a blender container and blend until smooth.
2. Allow to stand a few minutes to thicken before spooning over fresh fruit or other desserts.

I particularly like "Coconut" Sauce on pineapple.

Makes 1 cup sauce.

2 tablespoons contain approximately:
Free food, calories negligible
.2 mg. cholesterol
16 mg. sodium

Caribbean Rum Sauce

2 tablespoons corn oil margarine
2 tablespoons all-purpose flour
2 cups water, boiling

¼ cup fructose
1 teaspoon ground cinnamon
1 tablespoon vanilla extract
1 tablespoon dark rum

1. Melt the margarine in a saucepan.
2. Add the flour and cook, stirring constantly, for at least 3 minutes.
3. Remove the pan from the heat and add the boiling water all at once, stirring with a wire whisk.
4. Add the fructose and cinnamon to the pan and return the pan to the heat.
5. Simmer, stirring constantly with a wire whisk, until the sauce is slightly thickened.
6. Remove the pan from the heat and add the vanilla and dark rum.

Recipe continues . . .

199

This sauce is delicious served hot or cold. When serving it over Cold Banana Soufflé, I serve it cold. However, I like it better warm on most other things.

Makes 2 cups sauce.

2 tablespoons contain approximately:
   ½ fruit portion
   ¼ fat portion
   31 calories
   0 mg. cholesterol
   26 mg. sodium

Carob Sauce

2 tablespoons corn oil margarine

2 tablespoons all-purpose flour

2 cups water, boiling

½ cup carob powder

1½ teaspoons dry instant coffee

¼ cup fructose

1 tablespoon vanilla extract

1. Melt the margarine in a saucepan.
2. Add the flour and cook, stirring constantly, for at least 3 minutes.
3. Remove the pan from the heat and add the boiling water all at once, stirring with a wire whisk.
4. Add the carob powder, instant coffee and fructose to the pan and return the pan to the heat.
5. Simmer, stirring constantly with a wire whisk, until the sauce is slightly thickened.
6. Remove the pan from the heat and add the vanilla.

200

This sauce is the base for the Carob Sauce variations that follow.

Makes 2 cups sauce.

2 tablespoons contain approximately:
 ½ fruit portion
 ¼ fat portion
 31 calories
 0 mg. cholesterol
 26 mg. sodium

Jamaican Carob Sauce

2 cups Carob Sauce (preceding recipe)
1½ teaspoons rum extract, or 1 tablespoon dark rum

1. When making the basic Carob Sauce, add the rum extract or rum to the other ingredients for this tasty variation.

Makes 2 cups.

2 tablespoons contain approximately:
 ½ fruit portion
 ¼ fat portion
 31 calories
 0 mg. cholesterol
 26 mg. sodium

Crunchy Carob Sauce

½ cup raw almonds, finely chopped
2 cups Carob Sauce (see index)

1. Preheat the oven to 350°. Place the almonds on a cookie sheet in the center of the oven for 10 minutes, or until golden brown. Watch them carefully as they burn easily.
2. Combine the toasted almonds with the Carob Sauce and mix thoroughly.

Makes 2½ cups.

2 tablespoons contain approximately:
    ¼ fruit portion
    ½ fat portion
    43 calories
    0 mg. cholesterol
    21 mg. sodium

Beverages

Beverages range from cool, refreshing, tall drinks served over ice in frosted glasses to warming toddies served in mugs in front of the fire on cold evenings.

A beverage can also be practically calorie-free or a meal in a glass.

In this section you will find a bit of everything—even a Diet Bullet, which is a new calorie-cutting aid to people on the Fabulous Fructose Diet.

Desert Tea

2 quarts cold water
2 tea bags

1. Put the tea bags in a 2-quart glass jar or bottle, fill with water, and put the lid on the container. Put the jar in the sun until the tea is of the desired strength. This usually takes 2 hours, depending on the strength of the sun.
2. Remove the tea bags and store the tea in the refrigerator.

Makes 8 servings.

Recipe continues . . .

Each serving contains approximately:
Calories negligible.
0 mg. cholesterol
trace sodium

VARIATION: *Add grated orange rind or crushed mint leaves to the water at the same time you put in the tea bags.*

Low-Cholesterol Eggnog

2 cups liquid nonfat milk
2 egg whites
1 teaspoon vanilla extract
½ teaspoon rum extract
¼ teaspoon ground coriander
¼ teaspoon ground nutmeg

¼ teaspoon ground cinnamon
1 tablespoon liquid fructose
½ cup crushed ice
Ground nutmeg for garnish
Cinnamon sticks for garnish
  (optional)

1. Combine all ingredients, except nutmeg and cinnamon for garnish, in a blender container and blend until smooth and frothy.
2. Serve in chilled glasses. Sprinkle a little nutmeg on each serving. Garnish with cinnamon sticks if desired.

Makes 2 servings.

Each serving contains approximately:
1 nonfat milk portion
½ low-fat protein portion
¼ fruit portion
118 calories
1.1 mg. cholesterol
174 mg. sodium

Carob Caliente

(Breakfast in a mug)

1 cup liquid nonfat milk
1 tablespoon carob powder
1 teaspoon dry decaffeinated
   instant coffee
¼ teaspoon ground cinnamon
½ teaspoon vanilla extract
1 tablespoon unprocessed
   wheat bran

1 tablespoon defatted wheat
   germ
1 tablespoon liquid fructose
¼ cup low-fat cottage cheese
Cinnamon sticks for garnish
   (optional)

1. Put all ingredients except cinnamon sticks in a blender container and blend until completely smooth.
2. Pour the mixture into a saucepan and heat until warm. *Do not boil!*

This is a delicious, nutritious breakfast for people in a hurry in the morning.

Makes 2 servings.

Each serving contains approximately:
   ½ nonfat milk portion
   ½ starch portion
   ½ low-fat protein portion
   ½ fruit portion
   128 calories
   2.5 mg. cholesterol
   181 mg. sodium

VARIATION: *Carob Cooler: Add 4 ice cubes to the ingredients in the blender container and serve cold in tall glasses. This is also a uniquely different after-school snack for children.*

205

Counterfeit Cocktail

1 glass of soda water
Fresh lime or lemon juice to taste
Angostura bitters to taste

1. Pour the soda over ice in a tall glass or goblet.
2. Add lime or lemon juice and Angostura bitters to taste.
    I like to add enough Angostura bitters to my Counterfeit
Cocktail to make it a beautiful pale pink.

Makes 1 serving.

Each serving contains approximately:
    Free food, calories negligible
    0 mg. cholesterol
    trace sodium

Old-Fashioned Lemonade-Stand Lemonade

¾ cup freshly squeezed lemon juice
¼ cup liquid fructose
3 cups water

1. Combine lemon juice and fructose and mix well.
2. Add the water and again mix well.
3. Refrigerate until very cold before serving.
4. Serve over ice cubes in paper cups and sell to friends for 1
nickel.

Makes 1 quart lemonade.

1 cup contains approximately:
    1 fruit portion
    40 calories
    0 mg. cholesterol
    trace sodium

VARIATION: *Fancy French Lemonade: Use Perrier water in place of plain water.*

Ramos Fizzle

1 cup liquid nonfat milk
1 tablespoon liquid fructose
1 tablespoon fresh lemon juice
½ teaspoon orange-flower
    water

1 egg white
¼ cup club soda

1. Put all ingredients in a blender container and blend until smooth and frothy.
2. Pour over ice in 2 chilled tall glasses. Additional soda water may be added if desired.

Makes 2 servings.

Each serving contains approximately:
    ½ nonfat milk portion
    ½ fruit portion
    60 calories
    1.1. mg. cholesterol
    87 mg. sodium

Bloody Shame

(Without vodka, even without salt.)

2 tablespoons fresh lime juice
4 teaspoons fructose
½ teaspoon freshly ground
  black pepper
1½ cups (12 ounces) V-8 juice
  or tomato juice

4 to 6 drops of Tabasco, depending upon how hot you
  want it
Ice cubes
Raw zucchini or cucumber
  sticks, optional, for garnish

1. Mix the fresh lime juice, fructose and pepper until the fructose is dissolved.
2. Add juice and Tabasco to taste and mix well.
3. Pour over ice cubes and garnish with zucchini or cucumber sticks if desired.

Makes 2 servings.

Each serving contains approximately:
  ¾ fruit portion
  1 vegetable portion
  55 calories
  0 mg. cholesterol
  55 mg. sodium with low-sodium juice

Peanut Butter Punch

1 cup liquid nonfat milk
2 tablespoons unhomogenized
  unsalted peanut butter
1 tablespoon liquid fructose

1 teaspoon vanilla extract
½ cup crushed ice
Ground cinnamon or nutmeg
  for garnish (optional)

1. Put all ingredients except spice for garnish in a blender container and blend until smooth and frothy.
2. Pour into 2 chilled glasses and sprinkle a little cinnamon or nutmeg on top of each serving if desired.

Makes 2 servings.

Each serving contains approximately:
    ½ high-fat protein portion
    ½ nonfat milk portion
    ½ fruit portion
    108 calories
    1.1 mg. cholesterol
    67 mg. sodium

Tropical Fruit Smoothie

1 small banana, peeled and
    sliced
1 teaspoon fresh lemon juice
1 cup unsweetened pineapple
    juice
1 cup fresh orange juice
1 cup liquid nonfat milk

2 teaspoons liquid fructose
1 teaspoon vanilla extract
1 teaspoon coconut extract
½ cup crushed ice
Mint sprigs for garnish (op-
    tional)

1. Put all of the ingredients except mint sprigs in a blender container and blend until smooth and frothy.
2. Pour into 4 chilled glasses and garnish with fresh mint if desired.

Makes 4 servings.

Recipe continues . . .

209

Each serving contains approximately:
    ¼ nonfat milk portion
    2 fruit portions
    100 calories
    1.1 mg. cholesterol
    33 mg. sodium

Banana Breakfast Bullet

½ cup liquid nonfat milk
½ sliced banana, frozen
1 Diet Bullet packet*
¼ teaspoon vanilla extract

1. Combine all ingredients in a blender container and blend until smooth and frothy.

Makes 1 serving.

Each serving contains approximately:
    1 low-fat protein portion
    ½ nonfat milk portion
    1½ fruit portions
    128 calories
    1.1 mg. cholesterol
    66 mg. sodium

VARIATIONS: *1) One portion of any other fruit, frozen, may be used in place of bananas.*
2) A plain "Bullet" does not require a blender. It may be stirred directly into either nonfat milk or fruit juice. It dissolves immediately.

* This is an item packaged by Batter-Lite Foods, Inc., for people on the Fabulous Fructose Diet. See page 35 for additional information.

APPENDIXES

APPENDIXES

Appendix 1
Food Lists

Food Portions

(See lists for sizes of the portions)

Portion	Calories	Grams of Carbohydrate	Grams of Protein	Grams of Fat
Fruit	40	10		
Vegetable	25	5	2	
Starch	70	15	2	
Low-fat protein	55		7	3
Medium-fat protein	75		7	5
High-fat protein	95		7	7
Fat	45			5
Nonfat milk	80	12	8	Trace
Low-fat milk	125	12	8	5
Whole milk	170	12	8	10

Key to Abbreviations

gm fiber = grams of fiber
mg. chol. = milligrams cholesterol
mg. sodium = milligrams of sodium
tr. = trace

Fruit Portion List

Each portion below equals 1 Fruit Portion
and contains approximately:
10 grams of carbohydrate
40 calories

* good source of Vitamin C
** good source of Vitamin A
*** good source of Vitamins A and C
†† figures not available

gm fiber	mg. chol.	mg. sodium	
1.0	0	1	Apple: 1, 2 inches in diameter
.1	0	.7	Apple juice: ⅓ cup
.6	0	2	Applesauce, unsweetened: ½ cup
.6	0	1	Apricots, fresh: 2 medium**
.5	0	3	Apricots, dried: 3 halves**
			Avocado: see Fat Portion List
.3	0	.5	Banana: ½ small
2.0	0	1	Blackberries: ½ cup
1.1	0	1	Blueberries: ½ cup
.3	0	10	Cantaloupe: ¼, 6 inches in diameter***
.3	0	1	Cherries, sweet: 10 large
††	0	2	Cranberries, unsweetened: 1 cup
.3	0	††	Crenshaw melon: 2-inch wedge
.5	0	2	Dates: 2
.5	0	2	Date "sugar": 1 tablespoon

214

gm fiber	mg. chol.	mg. sodium	
.6	0	1	Figs, fresh: 1 large
.8	0	7	Figs, dried: 1 large
0	0	0	Fructose: 1 tablespoon
.2	0	1	Grapefruit: ½, 4 inches in diameter*
Tr.	0	1	Grapefruit juice: ½ cup*
.4	0	2	Grapes: 12 large
.2	0	2	Grapes, Thompson Seedless: 20 grapes
Tr.	0	1	Grape juice: ¼ cup
4.4	0	2	Guava: ⅔*
0	0	1	Honey: 2 teaspoons
.7	0	27	Honeydew melon: ¼, 5 inches in diameter
3.0	0	6	Kumquats: 2
Tr.	0	1	Lemon juice: ½ cup
Tr.	0	1	Lime juice: ½ cup
.5	0	††	Loquats: 3
.2	0	3	Litchi nuts, fresh: 3
.9	0	3	Mango: ½ small**
††	0	18	Molasses, blackstrap: 1 tablespoon
.3	0	8	Nectarine: 1 medium
.5	0	1	Orange: 1 small*
.1	0	1	Orange juice: ½ cup*
1.0	0	3	Papaya: ⅓ medium*
1.5	0	16	Passionfruit: 1
.1	0	††	Passionfruit juice: ⅓ cup
.6	0	1	Peach: 1 medium
1.0	0	3	Pear: 1 small
.8	0	3	Persimmon: ½ medium
.3	0	1	Pineapple, fresh or canned without sugar: ½ cup
Tr.	0	1	Pineapple juice: ⅓ cup
.2	0	6	Plantain: ½ small
.3	0	2	Plums: 2 medium
.2	0	3	Pomegranate: 1 small

215

gm fiber	mg. chol.	mg. sodium	
.3	0	2	Prunes, fresh or dried: 2
Tr.	0	5	Prune juice: ¼ cup
.2	0	6	Raisins: 2 tablespoons
3.0	0	1	Raspberries: ½ cup
1.5	0	1	Strawberries: ¾ cup
0	0	0	Sucrose: 1 tablespoon
.5	0	2	Tangerines: 1 large or 2 small
.5	0	1.5	Watermelon: ¾ cup

Vegetable Portion List

Each portion below equals 1 Vegetable Portion, is equal to 1 cup
unless otherwise specified, and contains approximately:
5 grams of carbohydrate
2 grams of protein
25 calories

*good source of Vitamin C
**good source of Vitamin A
***good source of Vitamins A and C
†calories negligible when eaten raw
††figures not available

gm fiber	mg. chol.	mg. sodium	
.6	0	††	Alfalfa sprouts†
4.8	0	40	Artichoke, whole, base and ends of leaves (1 small)
1.0	0	1	Asparagus†
.7	0	4	Bean sprouts†
.8	0	40	Beets (½ cup)

216

gm fiber	mg. chol.	mg. sodium	
1.3	0	37	Beet greens
††	0	8	Breadfruit (¼ cup)
1.5	0	22	Broccoli***†
1.6	0	16	Brussels sprouts*
.8	0	16	Cabbage*†
1.0	0	24	Carrots (medium), 1**
1.0	0	12	Cauliflower†
.6	0	100	Celery†
.7	0	100	Celery root (½ cup)
.9	0	166	Chard†
.8	0	12	Chayote
.9	0	††	Chicory**†
2.0	0	42	Chilies†
1.2	0	16	Chives***†
1.4	0	††	Cilantro†
.9	0	56	Collard*†
.6	0	8	Cucumber†
1.6	0	80	Dandelion greens†
1.8	0	2	Eggplant
1.2	0	10	Endive†
1.0	0	10	Escarole**†
††	0	10	Garlic (¼ cup)
.5	0	3	Green beans: see String beans
1.0	0	8	Green onion tops†
.5	0	††	Jerusalem artichokes (½ cup)
††	0	††	Jicama
1.2	0	48	Kale*†
.7	0	12	Leeks (½ cup)
.6	0	7	Lettuce†
1.8	0	.5	Lima beans, baby (¼ cup)
††	0	††	Mint†
.8	0	10	Mushrooms†
.9	0	12	Mustard, fresh*†

217

gm fiber	mg. chol.	mg. sodium	
1.0	0	4	Okra
.6	0	9	Onions (½ cup)
1.2	0	††	Palm heart
1.5	0	32	Parsley***†
.75	0	.4	Peas (¼ cup)
††	0	Tr.	Pea pods (½ cup)
1.5	0	20	Peppers, green and red*†
††	0	8	Pimiento (½ cup)
.9	0	††	Poke†
1.3	0	2	Pumpkin (½ cup)*
.7	0	20	Radishes†
.9	0	2	Rhubarb†
.7	0	4	Romaine lettuce†
1.1	0	4	Rutabagas (½ cup)
††	0	9	Shallots (½ cup)
.9	0	37	Spinach†
1.2	0	1	Squash, acorn (½ cup)
1.4	0	1	Squash, Hubbard (½ cup)
††	0	2	Squash, spaghetti
1.2	0	6	String beans
1.2	0	2	Summer squash†
.9	0	6	Tomatoes (1 medium)
††	0	15	Tomatoes, canned in juice, unsalted (½ cup)
.1	0	282	Tomato catsup, regular (1½ tablespoons)
††	0	6	Tomato catsup, dietetic, low-sodium (1½ tablespoons)
.4	0	244	Tomato juice (½ cup)
††	0	26	Tomato juice, unsalted (½ cup)
.3	0	186	Tomato paste (2 tablespoons)
††	0	12	Tomato paste, unsalted (3 tablespoons)
.6	0	831	Tomato sauce (½ cup)

gm fiber	mg. chol.	mg. sodium	
††	0	42	Tomato sauce, unsalted (½ cup)
.8	0	27	Turnips (½ cup)
.3	0	550	V-8 juice (⅔ cup)**
††	0	49	V-8 juice, unsalted (⅔ cup)**
.2	0	8	Water chestnuts (medium) (4)
.7	0	16	Watercress** †
1.4	0	1	Zucchini squash †

Starch Portion List

Each portion below equals 1 Starch Portion and
contains approximately:
15 grams of carbohydrate
2 grams of protein
70 calories

*good source of Vitamin A
†† figures not available

gm fiber	mg. chol.	mg. sodium	Vegetables
1.4	0	3	Beans, dried, cooked, unsalted (lima, soya, navy, pinto, kidney): ½ cup
.5	0	1.5	Beans, baked, without salt or pork: ¼ cup
.6	0	1	Corn, on-the-cob: 1, 4 inches long
.6	0	1	Corn, cooked and drained: ⅓ cup
.1	0	††	Hominy: ½ cup
.7	0	14	Lentils, dried, cooked: ½ cup
2.0	0	8	Parsnips: 1 small

219

gm fiber	mg. chol.	mg. sodium	
.5	0	13	Peas, dried, cooked (black-eyed, split): ½ cup
.7	0	7	Potatoes, sweet, yams: ¼ cup**
.5	0	2	Potatoes, white, baked or boiled: 1, 2 inches in diameter
.5	0	2	Potatoes, white, mashed: ½ cup
.2	0	300	Potato chips: 15, 2 inches in diameter
2.6	0	4	Pumpkin, canned: 1 cup
.2	0	6	Rice, brown, cooked, unsalted: ⅓ cup
Tr.	0	3	Rice, white, cooked, unsalted: ½ cup
††	0	4	Rice, wild, cooked, unsalted: ½ cup
.2	0	564	Tomato catsup, commercial: 3 table-spoons
††	0	12	Tomato catsup, dietetic low-sodium: 3 tablespoons

Breads

Tr.	0	††	Bagel: ½
Tr.	0	185	Biscuit: 1, 2 inches in diameter
††	0	7	Bread, low sodium: 1 slice
.1	0	139	Bread, rye: 1 slice
.4	0	136	Bread, whole wheat: 1 slice
Tr.	0	148	Bread (white and sourdough): 1 slice
Tr.	0	200	Breadsticks: 4, 7 inches long
Tr.	0	116	Bun, hamburger: ½
Tr.	0	153	Bun, hot dog: ⅔
.1	0	245	Corn bread: 1 piece 1½ inches square
.3	0	††	Cracked wheat (bulgur): 1½ tablespoons
Tr.	0	140	Croutons, plain: ½ cup
††	0	7	Croutons, plain, low-sodium bread: ½ cup

220

gm fiber	mg. chol.	mg. sodium	
Tr.	0	133	English muffin: ½
Tr.	0	1	Matzo cracker, plain: 1, 6 inches in diameter
Tr.	0	222	Melba toast: 6 slices
Tr.	0	117	Muffin, unsweetened: 1, 2 inches in diameter
Tr.	0	412	Pancakes: 2, 3 inches in diameter
††	0	7	Pancakes, low-sodium: 2, 3 inches in diameter
Tr.	0	88	Popover: 1
Tr.	0	143	Roll: 1, 2 inches in diameter
Tr.	0	70	Rusks: 2
.1	0	712	Spoon bread: ½ cup
.3	0	Tr.	Tortilla, corn, flour: 1, 7 inches in diameter
Tr.	0	203	Waffle: 1, 4 inches in diameter

Cereals

gm fiber	mg. chol.	mg. sodium	
2.4	0	287	All-Bran: ½ cup
2.0	0	94	Bran Flakes: ½ cup
3.3	0	††	Bran, unprocessed rice: ⅓ cup
3.2	0	††	Bran, unprocessed wheat: ⅓ cup
.2	0	240	Cheerios: 1 cup
.2	0	††	Concentrate: ¼ cup
.1	0	178	Corn Flakes: ⅔ cup
.1	0	1	Cornmeal, cooked: ½ cup
Tr.	0	1	Cream-of-Wheat, cooked: ½ cup
.4	0	147	Grapenuts: ¼ cup
.3	0	113	Grapenut Flakes: ½ cup
.1	0	1	Grits, cooked: ½ cup
Tr.	0	165	Kix: ¾ cup
.3	0	132	Life: ½ cup

gm fiber	mg. chol.	mg. sodium	
Tr.	0	1	Malt-O-Meal, cooked: ½ cup
Tr.	0	2	Maypo, cooked: ½ cup
Tr.	0	1	Matzo meal, cooked: ½ cup
.2	0	1	Oatmeal, cooked: ½ cup
.2	0	92	Pep: ½ cup
.2	0	1	Puffed rice: 1½ cups
.3	0	1	Puffed wheat: 1½ cups
Tr.	0	174	Rice Krispies: ⅔ cup
.4	0	1	Shredded wheat, biscuit: 1 large
.3	0	168	Special K: 1¼ cups
.2	0	1	Steel cut oats, cooked: ½ cup
.4	0	163	Wheat Chex: ½ cup
Tr.	0	1	Wheat germ, defatted: 1 ounce or 3 tablespoons
.2	0	210	Wheaties: ⅔ cup

Flours

Tr.	0	2	Arrowroot: 2 tablespoons
Tr.	0	1	All-purpose: 2½ tablespoons
Tr.	0	138	Bisquick: 1½ tablespoons
3.2	0	††	Bran, unprocessed wheat: 5 tablespoons
.3	0	1	Buckwheat: 3 tablespoons
Tr.	0	1	Cake: 2½ tablespoons
.1	0	Tr.	Cornmeal: 3 tablespoons
Tr.	0	Tr.	Cornstarch: 2 tablespoons
Tr.	0	1	Matzo meal: 3 tablespoons
Tr.	0	12	Potato flour: 2½ tablespoons
.5	0	1	Rye, dark: 4 tablespoons
.6	0	1	Whole-wheat: 3 tablespoons
Tr.	0	1	Noodles, macaroni, spaghetti, cooked: ½ cup

gm fiber	mg. chol.	mg. sodium	
Tr.	9.4	2	Noodles, dry, egg: 3½ ounces
Tr.	3.1	15	Noodles, cooked, egg: 3½ ounces

Crackers

gm fiber	mg. chol.	mg. sodium	
Tr.	0	††	Animal: 8
Tr.	0	33	Arrowroot: 3
Tr.	0	††	Cheese tidbits: ½ cup
.2	0	88	Graham: 2
††	0	10	Low-sodium: 4
Tr.	0	220	Oyster: 20 or ½ cup
Tr.	0	90	Pretzels: 10 very thin, or 1 large
Tr.	0	250	Saltines: 5, salted
Tr.	0	69	Soda: 3, unsalted
Tr.	0	192	Ritz: 6
.3	0	225	RyKrisp: 3
.3	0	130	Rye thins: 10
Tr.	0	336	Triangle thins: 14
††	0	150	Triscuits: 5
Tr.	0	††	Vegetable thins: 12
Tr.	0	276	Wheat thins: 12

Miscellaneous

gm fiber	mg. chol.	mg. sodium	
1.8	0	10	Cocoa, dry, unsweetened: 2½ tablespoons
††	0	120	Fritos: ¾ ounce or ½ cup
0	26.3	40	Ice cream, low-saturated fat: ½ cup
.3	0	1	Popcorn, popped, unbuttered and unsalted: 1½ cups

223

Low-fat Protein Portion List

Each portion below equals 1 Low-fat Protein Portion
and contains approximately:
7 grams of protein
3 grams of fat
55 calories

†† figures not available

gm fiber	mg. chol.	mg. sodium	Cheese
0	2.6	234	Cottage cheese, low-fat: ¼ cup
0	††	††	Cottage cheese, dry-curd: ¼ cup
0	††	222	Farmer's: ¼ cup, crumbled, salted
0	3.0	75	Farmer's: ¼ cup, crumbled, unsalted
0	3.0	††	Hoop: ¼ cup
0	3.0	12	Pot: ¼ cup
0	18.2	46	Ricotta, part skim: ¼ cup or 2 ounces

			Egg Substitutes
0	0	130	Liquid egg substitute: ¼ cup (sodium content varies with brands)
0	0	††	Dry egg substitute: 3 tablespoons

			Chicken
0	25.8	22	Broiled or roasted: 1 ounce or 1 slice 3 x 2 x ⅛ inches
0	22.4	19	Breast, without skin: ½ small, 1 ounce or ¼ cup, chopped
0	25.8	25	Leg: ½ medium or 1 ounce

224

gm fiber	mg. chol.	mg. sodium	Turkey
0	22.4	23	Meat, white, without skin: 1 ounce or 1 slice 3 x 2 x ⅛ inches
0	††	28	Meat, dark, without skin: 1 ounce or 1 slice 3 x 2 x ⅛ inches

Other Poultry and Game

0	30.0	25	Buffalo: 1 ounce or 1 slice 3 x 2 x ⅛ inches
0	††	22	Cornish game hen, without skin: ¼ bird or 1 ounce
0	††	20	Pheasant: 1½ ounces
0	††	12	Quail, without skin: ¼ bird or 1 ounce
0	25.8	18	Rabbit: 1 ounce or 1 slice 3 x 2 x ⅛ inches
0	††	22	Squab, without skin: ¼ bird or 1 ounce
0	††	25	Venison, lean, roast or steak: 1 ounce or 1 slice 3 x 2 x ⅛ inches

Fish and Seafood

0	24.4	††	Abalone: 1⅓ ounces
0	18.3	112	Albacore, canned in oil: 1 ounce
0	21.4	††	Anchovy fillets: 9
0	††	1540	Anchovy paste: 1 tablespoon
0	27.1	15	Bass: 1½ ounces
0	85.7	624	Caviar: 1 ounce
0	18.0	51	Clams, fresh: 3 large or 1½ ounces
0	27.0	††	Clams, canned: 1½ ounces
0	††	††	Clam juice: 1½ cups
0	18.1	31	Cod: 1 ounce
0	43.0	77	Crab, canned: ½ ounce

225

gm fiber	mg. chol.	mg. sodium	
0	42.5	90	Crab, cracked, fresh: 1½ ounces
0	30.2	110	Flounder: 1⅔ ounces
0	55.0	††	Frog legs: 2 large or 3 ounces
0	18.1	30	Halibut: 1 ounce or 1 piece 2 x 2 x 1 inch
0	27.0	††	Herring, pickled: 1¼ ounces
0	††	2207	Herring, smoked: 1¼ ounces
0	31.0	90	Lobster, fresh: 1½ ounces, ¼ cup or ¼ small lobster
0	36.0	90	Lobster, canned, unsalted: 1½ ounces
0	23.0	31	Oysters, fresh: 3 medium or 1½ ounces
0	25.5	171	Oysters, canned: 1½ ounces
0	27.1	39	Perch: 1½ ounces
0	27.1	38	Red snapper: 1½ ounces
0	18.4	14	Salmon: 1 ounce
0	16.0	235	Salmon, canned: 1½ ounces
0	24.4	33	Sand dabs: 1½ ounces
0	40.0	108	Sardines: 4 small
0	††	26	Sardines, unsalted: 4 small
0	23.0	112	Scallops: 3 medium or 1½ ounces
0	30.0	44	Sole: 1⅔ ounces
0	48.0	60	Shrimp, fresh: 5 medium
0	64.0	††	Shrimp, canned: 5 medium or 1½ ounces
0	27.1	††	Swordfish: 1½ ounces
0	27.1	11	Trout: 1½ ounces
0	18.1	10	Tuna, fresh: 1 ounce
0	††	370	Tuna, canned in oil: ¼ cup
0	††	25	Tuna, unsalted, water packed (dietetic): ¼ cup
0	27.1	32	Turbot: 1½ ounces

226

gm fiber	mg. chol.	mg. sodium	Beef
0	41.8	26	Flank steak: 1½ ounces
0	31.3	17	Rib roast: 1 ounce, ¼ cup, chopped, or 1 slice 3 x 2 x ⅛ inches
0	30.0	17	Steak, very lean (filet mignon, New York, sirloin, T-bone): 1 ounce or 1 slice 3 x 2 x ⅛ inches
0	††	21	Tripe: 1 ounce or 1 piece 5 x 2 inches

Lamb

gm fiber	mg. chol.	mg. sodium	
0	28.0	20	Chops, lean: ½ small chop or 1 ounce
0	27.7	20	Roast, lean: 1 ounce, 1 slice 3 x 2 x ⅛ inches, or ¼ cup, chopped

Pork

gm fiber	mg. chol.	mg. sodium	
0	25.3	264	Ham: 1 ounce or 1 slice 3 x 2 x ⅛ inches

Veal

gm fiber	mg. chol.	mg. sodium	
0	28.7	23	Chop: ½ small or 1 ounce
0	29.0	23	Cutlet: 1 ounce or 1 slice 3 x 2 x ⅛ inches
0	28.7	23	Roast: 1 ounce or 1 slice 3 x 2 x ⅛ inches

227

Medium-fat Protein Portion List

Each portion below equals 1 Medium-fat Protein Portion
and contains approximately:
7 grams of protein
5 grams of fat
75 calories

gm fiber	mg. chol.	mg. sodium	Cheese
0	8.4	130	Cottage cheese, creamed: ¼ cup
0	16.0	††	Feta: 1 ounce
0	17.4	227	Mozzarella: 1 ounce
0	14.8	163	Parmesan: ¼ cup, ⅔ ounce, or 4 table-spoons
0	29.1	46	Ricotta, regular: ¼ cup or 2 ounces
0	14.8	247	Romano: ¼ cup, ⅔ ounce, or 4 table-spoons

			Eggs
0	250.0	59	Eggs, medium: 1
0	0	47	Egg white: 1 (does not constitute a whole portion)
0	250.0	12	Egg yolk: 1 (does not constitute a whole portion)

			Chicken
0	††	16	Gizzard: 1 ounce
0	††	20	Heart: 1 ounce
0	211.4	17	Liver: 1 ounce

gm fiber	mg. chol.	mg. sodium	Beef
0	571.4	54	Brains: 1 ounce
0	26.0	298	Corned beef, canned: 1 ounce or 1 slice 3 x 2 x ⅛ inches
0	30.3	14	Hamburger, very lean (4 ounces raw-3 ounces cooked): 1 ounce
0	42.8	30	Heart: 1 ounce or 1 slice 3 x 2 x ⅛ inches
0	107.1	72	Kidney: 1 ounce or 1 slice 3 x 2 x ⅛ inches
0	124.1	59	Liver: 1 ounce or 1 slice 3 x 2 x ⅛ inches
0	††	17	Tongue: 1 slice 3 x 2 x ¼ inches

Pork

gm fiber	mg. chol.	mg. sodium	
0	25.3	343	Canadian bacon: 1 slice 2½ inches in diameter, ¼ inch thick
0	25.0	18	Chops, lean: ½ small chop or 1 ounce
0	††	19	Heart: 1 ounce
0	124.1	30	Liver: 1 ounce
0	25.0	18	Roast, lean: 1 ounce, 1 slice 3 x 2 x ⅛ inches, or ¼ cup, chopped

Veal

gm fiber	mg. chol.	mg. sodium	
0	124.1	30	Calf's liver: 1 ounce or 1 slice 3 x 2 x ⅛ inches
0	71.4	33	Sweetbreads: 1 ounce, ¼ pair, or ¼ cup, chopped
0	28.7	22	Roast, lean: 1 ounce, ¼ cup, chopped, or 1 slice 3 x 2 x ⅛ inches

229

High-fat Protein Portion List

Each portion below equals 1 High-fat Protein Portion
and contains approximately:
7 grams of protein
7 grams of fat
95 calories

†† figures not available

gm fiber	mg. chol.	mg. sodium	Cheese
0	28.4	193	American: 1 ounce
0	21.16	510	Bleu: 1 ounce or ¼ cup, crumbled
0	30.1	193	Cheddar: 1 ounce
0	††	10	Cheddar, low-sodium: 1 ounce (sodium content varies with brands)
0	29.1	204	Edam: 1 ounce
0	21.0	271	Liederkranz: 1 ounce
0	18.0	204	Monterey Jack: 1 ounce
0	25.0	204	Muenster: 1 ounce
Tr.	18.2	465	Pimiento cheese spread: 1 ounce
0	24.0	465	Roquefort: 1 ounce or ¼ cup, crumbled
0	21.0	††	Stilton: 1 ounce or ¼ cup, crumbled
0	28.0	85	Swiss: 1 ounce

gm fiber	mg. chol.	mg. sodium	Cold Cuts
0	25.9	266	Bologna: 1 ounce or 1 slice 4½ inches in diameter, ⅛ inch thick
0	††	264	Liverwurst: 1 slice 3 inches in diameter, ¼ inch thick
0	25.9	340	Spam: 1 ounce

gm fiber	mg. chol.	mg. sodium	
0	25.9	425	Salami: 1 ounce or 1 slice 4 inches in diameter, ⅓ inch thick
0	25.9	228	Vienna sausage: 2½ sausages or 1 ounce

Duck

0	††	21	Roasted, without skin: 1 ounce or 1 slice 3 x 2 x ⅛ inches
0	††	28	Wild duck, without skin: 1 ounce

Beef

0	31.3	17	Brisket: 1 ounce
0	25.9	508	Frankfurters: 1 (8 to 9 per pound)
0	31.3	18	Short ribs, very lean: 1 rib or 1 ounce

Peanut Butter

.3	0	156	Peanut butter, regular: 2 tablespoons
.3	0	6	Peanut butter, unsalted: 2 tablespoons

Pork

			Bacon: see Fat Portion List
0	25.9	250	Sausage: 2 small or 1 ounce
0	25.3	19	Spareribs, without fat: meat from 3 medium or 1 ounce

Fat Portion List

Each portion below equals 1 Fat Portion and
contains approximately:
5 grams of fat
45 calories

†† figures not available

gm fiber	mg. chol.	mg. sodium	
.8	0	1	Avocado: ⅛, 4 inches in diameter
0	7.0	209	Bacon, crisp: 1 slice
0	12.0	39	Butter: 1 teaspoon
0	††	.3	Butter, unsalted: 1 teaspoon
1.2	††	5	Caraway seeds: 2 tablespoons
1.2	††	5	Cardamom seeds: 2 tablespoons
0	0	4	Chocolate, bitter: ⅓ ounce or ⅓ square
0	10.0	35	Cream cheese: 1 tablespoon
0	20.0	12	Cream, light, coffee: 2 tablespoons
0	20.0	5	Cream, heavy, whipping: 1 tablespoon
0	17.0	18	Cream, half-and-half: 3 tablespoons
0	16.0	12	Cream, sour: 2 tablespoons
0	0	32	Cream, sour, imitation: 2 tablespoons Imo, Matey)
0	0	35	Margarine, polyunsaturated: 1 teaspoon
0	0	.8	Margarine, polyunsaturated, unsalted: 1 teaspoon
0	2.6	25	Mayonnaise: 1 teaspoon
0	0	0	Oils, polyunsaturated: 1 teaspoon
.6	††	125	Olives, ripe: 5 small
††	††	384	Olives, green: 4 medium
.8	††	3	Poppy seeds: 1½ tablespoons
.2	††	††	Pumpkin seeds: 1½ teaspoons

232

gm fiber	mg. chol.	mg. sodium	
			Salad dressings, commercial
Tr.	††	59	Bleu cheese: 1 teaspoon
Tr.	††	95	Bleu cheese, diet, sugar-free: 1 teaspoon
Tr.	††	57	Caesar: 1 teaspoon
Tr.	††	77	French: 1 teaspoon
Tr.	††	74	Italian: 1 teaspoon
Tr.	††	64	Italian, diet: 1 teaspoon
Tr.	††	48	Roquefort: 1 teaspoon
Tr.	††	44	Thousand island, diet: 1 teaspoon
Tr.	††	33	Thousand island, egg-free: 1 teaspoon
			Sauces, commercial
Tr.	††	††	Béarnaise: 1 teaspoon
Tr.	††	28	Hollandaise: 1 teaspoon
Tr.	††	61	Tartar sauce: 1 teaspoon
.2	0	4	Sesame seeds: 2 teaspoons
.2	0	3	Sunflower seeds: 1½ teaspoons

Nuts, Unsalted

gm fiber	mg. chol.	mg. sodium	
.3	0	.5	Almonds: 7
.2	0	.5	Brazil nuts: 2
.2	0	2	Cashews: 7
.5	0	5	Coconut, fresh: 1 piece 1 x 1 x ⅜ inches
.3	0	5	Coconut, shredded, unsweetened: 2 tablespoons
1.2	0	.5	Filberts: 5
1.2	0	.5	Hazelnuts: 5
.1	0	††	Hickory nuts: 7 small
.3	0	††	Macadamia nuts: 2
.4	0	1	Peanuts, Spanish: 20
.4	0	1	Peanuts, Virginia: 10
.3	0	Tr.	Pecans: 6 halves
.2	0	††	Pine nuts: 1 tablespoon

gm fiber	mg. chol.	mg. sodium	
.1	0	††	Pistachio nuts: 15
.2	0	††	Soy nuts, toasted: 3 tablespoons
.2	0	.5	Walnuts, black: 5 halves
.2	0	.5	Walnuts, California: 5 halves

Nonfat Milk Portion List

Each portion below equals 1 Nonfat Milk Portion
and contains approximately:
12 grams of carbohydrate
8 grams of protein
trace of fat
80 calories

gm fiber	mg. chol.	mg. sodium	
0	7.8	280	Buttermilk: 1 cup
0	††	155	Milk, powdered, skim, dry: 3 tablespoons
0	1.7	115	Milk, powdered, skim, mixed: ¼ cup
0	††	6	Milk, powdered, low-sodium (Featherweight): 3 tablespoons, dry, or 1 cup, mixed
0	2.3	127	Milk, skim, nonfat: 1 cup
0	††	121	Milk, skim, instant: 1 cup
0	2.3	165	Milk, evaporated, skim: ½ cup
0	††	75	Sherbet: 1 cup
0	††	116	Yogurt, plain, nonfat: 1 cup

Low-fat Milk Portion List

Each portion below equals 1 Low-fat Milk Portion
and contains approximately:
12 grams of carbohydrate
8 grams of protein
5 grams of fat
125 calories

gm fiber	mg. chol.	mg. sodium	
0	15.5	150	Milk, low-fat, 2% fat: 1 cup
0	††	12.5	Milk, Carnation Lo-Sodium Modified: 1 cup
0	17.0	115	Yogurt, plain, low-fat: 1 cup
0	††	141	Yogurt, flavored, low-fat: 1 cup

Whole Milk Portion List

Each portion below equals 1 Whole Milk Portion
and contains approximately:
12 grams of carbohydrate
8 grams of protein
10 grams of fat
170 calories

gm fiber	mg. chol.	mg. sodium	
0	26.0	136	Ice milk: 1 cup
0	32.7	120	Milk, whole: 1 cup
0	32.7	149	Milk, evaporated, whole: ½ cup

235

gm fiber	mg. chol.	mg. sodium	
0	††	6	Milk, low-sodium Lonolac liquid: 1 cup
0	††	114	Yogurt, plain, whole: 1 cup

Herbs, Spices, Seasonings, Etc.

Calories are negligible and need not be counted in the following list; however, many of these foods are extremely high in sodium and must be calculated very carefully.

gm fiber	mg. chol.	mg. sodium	
0	0	250	Baking Powder: 1 teaspoon
0	0	Tr.	Baking Powder, low-sodium: 1 teaspoon
0	0	1360	Baking Soda: 1 teaspoon
††	0	10	Bakon Yeast: 1 teaspoon (12 calories)
0	0	Tr.	Bitters, Angostura: 1 teaspoon
0	0	425	Bouillon cube, beef (fat-free): one ½-inch cube or 4 grams
0	0	10	Bouillon cube, beef (fat-free and salt-free): one ½-inch cube or 4 grams
0	0	5	Bouillon cube, chicken (fat-free and salt-free): one ½-inch cube or 4 grams
Tr.	0	306	Capers: 1 tablespoon
††	0	294	Chutney: 1 tablespoon (Crosse & Blackwell's Major Grey's)
0	0	1	Coffee: 1 cup
0	0	Tr.	Extracts: 1 teaspoon
0	0	4	Gelatin unsweetened: 1 envelope (1 scant tablespoon)
0	0	0	Liquid smoke: 1 teaspoon

236

gm fiber	mg. chol.	mg. sodium	
Tr.	0	63	Mustard, prepared: 1 teaspoon (French's)
Tr.	0	811	Pickles: 1, 2 ounce, without sugar
0	0	6	Rennet tablets: 1 ounce
0	0	2200	Salt: 1 teaspoon
0	0	2077	Soy sauce: 1 ounce (2 tablespoons)
0	0	6	Tabasco: ¼ teaspoon
0	0	Tr.	Vinegar, cider: 1 tablespoon
0	0	5	Vinegar, red-wine: 1 tablespoon
0	0	5	Vinegar, white-wine: 1 tablespoon
0	0	58	Worcestershire sauce: 1 tablespoon (Lea & Perrins)

Herbs and Spices

gm fiber	mg. chol.	mg. sodium	
.4	0	2	Allspice, ground: 1 teaspoon
.4	0	1	Allspice, whole: 1 teaspoon
††	0	Tr.	Aniseed: 1 teaspoon
.2	0	Tr.	Basil: 1 teaspoon
††	0	Tr.	Bay leaf: 1 leaf
.2	0	4	Celery seed, ground: 1 teaspoon
.2	0	2	Celery seed, whole: 1 teaspoon
††	0	31	Chili powder, seasoned: 1 teaspoon
.3	0	Tr.	Cinnamon, ground: 1 teaspoon
††	0	3	Cloves, ground: 1 teaspoon
††	0	1	Cloves, whole: 1 teaspoon
.4	0	Tr.	Coriander, ground: 1 teaspoon
.1	0	Tr.	Cuminseed: 1 teaspoon
††	0	1	Curry powder: 1 teaspoon
.4	0	Tr.	Dill seed: 1 teaspoon
††	0	Tr.	Dill weed: 1 teaspoon
.4	0	1	Fennel seed: 1 teaspoon
Tr.	0	1	Garlic powder: 1 teaspoon
††	0	1	Ginger, ground: 1 teaspoon

237

gm fiber	mg. chol.	mg. sodium	
††	0	Tr.	Juniper berries: 1
††	0	Tr.	Lemon peel, dried: 1 teaspoon
††	0	Tr.	Lemon peel, fresh: 1 teaspoon
Tr.	0	2	Mace, ground: 1 teaspoon
Tr.	0	Tr.	Marjoram, dried: 1 teaspoon
Tr.	0	Tr.	Mint, dried: 1 teaspoon
††	0	Tr.	Mustard seed: 1 teaspoon
Tr.	0	Tr.	Nutmeg, ground: 1 teaspoon
.1	0	2	Onion powder: 1 teaspoon
††	0	Tr.	Orégano, dried: 1 teaspoon
.4	0	1	Paprika, ground: 1 teaspoon
.1	0	5	Parsley flakes: 1 teaspoon
.2	0	Tr.	Pepper, black: 1 teaspoon
††	0	Tr.	Pepper, cayenne: 1 teaspoon
††	0	698	Pepper, lemon: 1 teaspoon (Durkee's)
.1	0	Tr.	Pepper, white: 1 teaspoon
.2	0	Tr.	Rosemary, dried: 1 teaspoon
††	0	Tr.	Saffron, powdered: 1 teaspoon
.1	0	Tr.	Sage, dried: 1 teaspoon
.2	0	Tr.	Savory, dried: 1 teaspoon
.1	0	Tr.	Tarragon, dried: 1 teaspoon
.1	0	Tr.	Thyme, dried: 1 teaspoon
.1	0	1	Turmeric, ground: 1 teaspoon

Alcoholic Beverages

Whether you are allowed alcoholic beverages in your diet should be decided between you and your doctor. There is no question that weight loss/maintenance is simplified greatly by not drinking, as liquor of all types is high in calories. Also, as you will notice by the figures given, many alcoholic beverages are also high in sodium.

A good way to think of a cocktail, highball or glass of wine is to visualize the drink as a slice of bread with a pat of butter on it. This image helps me more to refrain from having another drink than anything else does.

There is another problem with drinking on a restricted diet. Alcohol can lead to waiting too long before eating, eating too much, or eating something forbidden on the diet. Most doctors, however, consider cooking with wines completely acceptable. Wine adds very little food value to each portion, and all the alcohol is cooked away before the food is eaten.

Key to Abbreviations

C = calories
GC = grams of carbohydrate

gm fiber	mg. chol.	mg. sodium	
0	0	17	Ale, mild, 8 oz. = 98 C, 8 GC
0	0	8	Beer, 8 oz. = 114 C, 11 GC

Wines

0	0	3	Champagne, brut, 3 oz. = 75 C, 1 GC
0	0	3	Champagne, extra dry, 3 oz. = 87 C, 4 GC
0	0	4	Dubonnet, 3 oz. = 96 C, 7 GC
0	0	4	Dry Marsala, 3 oz. = 162 C, 18 GC
0	0	4	Sweet Marsala, 3 oz. = 182 C, 23 GC
0	0	4	Muscatel, 4 oz. = 158 C, 14 GC
0	0	4	Port, 4 oz. = 158 C, 14 GC
0	0	4	Red wine, dry, 3 oz. = 70 C, under 1 GC
0	0	4	Sake, 3 oz. = 75 C, 6 GC
0	0	4	Sherry, domestic, 3½ oz. = 84 C, 5 GC
0	0	4	Dry vermouth, 3½ oz. = 105 C, 1 GC

gm fiber	mg. chol.	mg. sodium	
0	0	4	Sweet vermouth, 3½ oz. = 167 C, 12 GC
0	0	4	White wine, dry, 3 oz. = 70 C, under 1 GC

Liqueurs and Cordials

0	0	2	Amaretto, 1 oz. = 112 C, 13 GC
0	0	2	Crème de Cacao, 1 oz. = 101 C, 12 GC
0	0	2	Crème de Menthe, 1 oz. = 112 C, 13 GC
0	0	2	Curacao, 1 oz. = 100 C, 9 GC
0	0	2	Drambuie, 1 oz. = 110 C, 11 GC
0	0	2	Tia Maria, 1 oz. = 113 C, 9 GC

Spirits

Bourbon, brandy, Cognac, Canadian whisky, gin, rye, rum, Scotch, tequila and vodka are all carbohydrate free! The calories they contain depend upon the proof.

0	0	Tr.	80 proof, 1 oz. = 67 C
0	0	Tr.	84 proof, 1 oz. = 70 C
0	0	Tr.	90 proof, 1 oz. = 75 C
0	0	Tr.	94 proof, 1 oz. = 78 C
0	0	Tr.	97 proof, 1 oz. = 81 C
0	0	Tr.	100 proof, 1 oz. = 83 C

Appendix 2
Basal Caloric Needs

WOMEN In order to calculate your approximate caloric needs, multiply your ideal body weight in pounds by 16. For example, a woman with an ideal weight of 100 pounds would require 1,600 calories per day unless she were pregnant, lactating, chemically abnormal, or unusually underactive or overactive. Or you can multiply your ideal body weight in kilograms by 35 to obtain the same caloric requirement.

MEN For the average-sized man, multiply your ideal body weight in pounds by 18. For example, a man with an ideal weight of 150 pounds would require 2,700 calories per day. (If kilograms are used, multiply your ideal body weight by 40 to get your caloric needs.) Very active men might require considerably more (25 calories per pound) and sedentary men might need only 13 or 14 calories per pound.

These figures are only approximate ones. The true test of a maintenance diet is whether a daily level of caloric intake will maintain the body weight within a certain tolerable limit over a period of months and years. Figures are for mature men and women in good health and in the age groups of 25 to 35. Older and younger persons will have slightly different requirements, but these figures will be close enough for the majority of those trying the FFD.

SOURCE: Health and Welfare Canada. Reproduced by permission of the Minister of Supply and Services Canada.

Appendix 3
Advice on Buying
Fructose Products

Although fructose is used to supplement many foods—dietetic and otherwise—pure fructose products are not common. Finding them often requires careful reading of labels and of product information.

It is important, however, to find these products because fructose loses its advantages when combined with other sugars. Therefore, if a label says "high in fructose" or "enriched with fructose" do not buy it. Also be careful of products that contain a mixture of fructose and protein, along with other food items.

Soft drinks now contain a syrup that is 55 percent fructose, but this amount is too low to be a true fructose product. Never use a product like this with less than a 90 percent fructose content.

The most economical way to buy fructose is as fructose-90 syrup, in chewable tablets or in premeasured packets. Always buy it in the pure form without additives or other food products. One exception is the premeasured packets of casein-lactalbumin-fructose, but these are only available through a doctor.

Appendix 4
Suppliers and
Information Sources

This list of suppliers of fructose products is not intended to be complete. It is a list of suppliers of acceptable products known to the author at the time of the writing of this book. In addition, no endorsement of any of these companies and their products is intended.

When writing these companies, enclose a stamped, self-addressed envelope and request any information they may have. Some will send you catalogs, and others publish recipe booklets showing how to use their products.

Suppliers of Fructose Products

Batter-Lite Foods, Inc.
P.O. Box 476
Beloit, Wisconsin 53511 (1 through 13, 15)

Control Drug, Inc.
230 Boiling Springs Avenue
East Rutherford, New Jersey 07073
Sales to doctors only
1-800-631-8373 (2)

The Estee Corporation
169 Lackawana Avenue
Parsippany, New Jersey 07054 (1, 2, 5, 6, 7, 9, 10, 12, 14, 15)

Earthquest Ltd.
3100 Maple Drive
Atlanta, Georgia 30305 (5, 8)

General Nutrition Corporation
921 Penn Avenue
Pittsburgh, Pennsylvania 15230 (2, 5, 9, 11, 15)

Lanpar-Parmae Co.
Sales to doctors only (2, 8)
1-800-527-9425

Miller Pharmaceutical Co.
Sales to doctors only
1-800-323-2935 (2, 8)

North Nassau Dispensary
1691 Northern Boulevard
Manhasset, New York 11030 (9)

Pfanstiehl Laboratories, Inc.
1219 Glen Rock Avenue
Waukegan, Illinois 60085 (2, 5, 15)

Sanavita Corp.
Suite 1006
575 Madison Avenue
New York, New York 10022 (2, 4, 5, 10, 12)

Vitose Corp.
154 Burlington
P.O. Drawer D
Clarendon Hills, Illinois 60514 (2, 15)

C. G. Whitlock Process Co.
P.O. Box 259
Springfield, Illinois 62705 (4, 11, 12)

Codes for Fructose Products
1. Cake and cookie mixes
2. Chewable tablets
3. Chewable tablets, flavored
4. Cookbooks
5. Direct mail sales to consumers
6. Drink mixes, iced tea and lemonade
7. Frosting mixes
8. Fructose/protein formula
9. Granules in premeasured packets and in bulk
10. Jams, jellies and preserves
11. Liquid sweetener
12. Liquid sweetener, honey flavored
13. Mayonnaise
14. Puddings and gelatins, fructose-based
15. Sold in stores

Appendix 5
Beware the Feeder

During the holiday seasons, and for that matter any time of year, you must be on the lookout for a vicious creature that preys on dieters, *the feeder*. They come in all shapes, sizes, and ages, but they have one common characteristic—they will try to wreck your diet.

Their motivations differ, but the results are the same—another diet down the drain. The purpose of this note is to make you aware that feeders exist, of some of their reasons for ruining your diet, and of how you can deal with them.

Feeders are more likely to be female, although there are some male feeders. The thin feeder is either normal weight or slightly overweight. The presence of someone fat makes this person look thinner. If a fat friend starts losing weight, a little bit of jealousy comes into the picture, and this feeder is apt to try to sabotage the dieter's efforts to lose.

The fat feeder may have several reasons for feeding you. She may not want you to look better than she does, or she may miss you as an eating buddy. She usually will not go to an ice cream parlor or a restaurant specializing in starchy foods unless she can go with a group of people. It is not as embarrassing to overeat if you are in a group. All of a sudden you no longer want to go to those places, and it makes her uncomfortable. The result is that she will try to tempt you to get back into her group of overeaters.

The last type of feeder is the grandparent figure. He or she may not be a grandparent, but the motivation is the same. This is a person who shows love by feeding someone. Anyone who doesn't accept this "love" by eating what is offered makes this feeder uncomfortable, to the point where she/he will almost demand that you go off your diet to please her/him.

All three types of feeders use the same tactics, some direct and some very subtle. Inviting you for dinner and then having nothing you can eat without going off your diet is a favorite trick, as is having you for a bridge game and pointedly placing a plate of dessert in front of you without giving you a chance to refuse. A good tactic is to tell a feeder in advance that you can only eat special foods and that you would like to bring your own supplies with you. The understanding friend will go along with this and accept that you are on a rigid diet. Never let yourself be caught away from home at the mercy of a feeder. Refuse invitations if known feeders are involved.

You don't have to be a social outcast, but certain environmental influences are deadly to a diet. A good idea is to stay away from church suppers, banquets, family reunions, and holiday parties unless you can bring your own supply of food. If this is impossible, then attend the function after the food is served or leave before the food is served if the food is the last thing on the program.

One favorite tactic of feeders is to remark how bad, how wrinkled, how much older, or even how good you look. The remark is then followed by their saying that you don't need to lose any more weight. One good response is to say, "What is your purpose in telling me this?" A feeder usually will be unable to answer, or she/he may say that she/he is just concerned about you. If she/he says the latter, tell her/him that the doctor has advised you that this weight loss is important for your present and future health, and that the doctor will tell you when to quit.

If the feeder tries to get you to eat, particularly something outrageously wrong, such as pie or cake, simply say, "My doctor told me that someone might try to get me off my diet, and he told me to say that I can't go off even a little bit." The usual response that a feeder makes to this is to say, "Oh, come on! A little bit of this won't hurt you." The thing that will shut up almost all feeders completely at this point is to say, "Well, my doctor said you might say that, too. He said if there were any question about whether I could eat it, then I am to get him on the phone and let you talk to him." This approach, along with a move toward the phone, will usually make the feeder leave you alone.

Remember one other thing as you progress on the weight-loss program: *You owe no one any explanation or apology for going on a diet and helping your health and appearance.*

One last thing about dealing with feeders. Know who your friends really are. People who knowingly try to get you off your diet are not your friends. They are either malicious or ignorant, or both. In none of these cases do you need to work with, socialize with, or deal with this type of person. Put them behind you if their attitude doesn't change and stay away from them. You will find there are many other people in the world who aren't like this, and among this better group of people are those who can fill the gap left by amputating the feeders from your group of friends.

Appendix 6
An Open Letter to the Spouse (or Parent or Friend) of My Patients

You may think this is rather an unconventional thing to do, appealing to someone close to a dieter for help, but certain things need to be said to you or all of the dieter's efforts will be for naught, and the dieter will fail. For this reason, please carefully read everything that follows. All the things mentioned below do not apply in every case, but they are used as an example of things that could go wrong.

It is obvious that no one holds an overweight person down and makes him eat. In 99 percent of the cases, the person who is overweight is that way because he eats more food than he burns. What is not so obvious is the effect that the environment has on the overweight individual. Numerous scientific experiments have pointed out time and time again that the surroundings and external influences on a fat person have more to do with his problem eating behavior than the internal cues of hunger can ever have.

A large majority of overweight persons never experience a true feeling of hunger or of satiety (lack of hunger) as an individual of normal weight does. These experiments have shown that cues such as elapsed time from the most recent meals, smell, sight of food, activities usually associated with food (watching TV and eating), being in a certain location, and emotional upset will trigger massive food intake. These cues can make even the most compliant dieter vulnerable.

You may be asking yourself, "What does all this have to do with me? It isn't my problem. He or she should be able to diet by will power! Why involve me at all? If he can't do well, it is his weakness."

Nothing could be further from the truth. You are important, in fact more important than most of the people in the dieter's life, or you would not be reading this letter. If you are truly interested in helping the dieter, please take what is said here on faith for a while and see for yourself whether or not it is true. It may mean changing your own life-style a bit, but the results will be worthwhile.

To begin with, please never criticize the dieter for not dieting or for his or her eating habits. Ridicule, teasing, taunting, or other verbal abuse does not stop an undesirable behavior. It most likely will only make the overweight person want to eat more. You may have to bite your tongue to do so, but only comment on desirable behavior. If the patient is not breaking his or her diet, then comment on how good he or she is. If a lapse does occur, and this will happen, the less said the better. In the long run, positive reinforcement techniques work better for compliance to a diet. To repeat, even if you see something done wrong, please say nothing.

Since visual or olfactory cues are important in producing undesirable eating behavior, the dieter needs to fat-proof his dwelling. This means the cleaning out of all junk food that might tempt him. For the rest of your family, it may mean going out to get ice cream and not eating it or something equally tempting in front of the dieter. To eat such goodies in front of a dieter is the height of cruelty.

Many families are used to eating together, but the dieter may decide not to eat with you if he or she is bothered by sitting and watching others eat. He or she may simply take his or her meals and then get up right after finishing, even if others have not yet stopped eating. Many dieters are pickers, and if such a person remains at the table, he/she will find something to nibble on. Please be understanding, and at a later date when dieting efforts have been successful, the normal table behavior will be resumed.

A dieter may have to stay away from problem places, such as pizza parlors, taco stands, spaghetti houses, hamburger stands, take-out chicken stores, doughnut stores, and other equally tempting dens of obesity for dieters. Please don't bring this type of food home and tempt the dieter. The result is usually disastrous and is equivalent to tempting an alcoholic to go into a bar or bringing him a bottle of whiskey. No one in his right mind would do that to an alcoholic, but lots of people will try to "feed" a dieter.

What this message boils down to is that the dieter is weak and does have some bad habits, but he is worth any and all efforts to help save him from the life-shortening effects of obesity. You and others may be inconvenienced a little, but surely you can tolerate these minor annoyances for a while.

About one out of every hundred dieters is faced with overt or covert sadism or mental illness on the part of his or her spouse or a relative.

A certain type of person seems to feed on the misery of others, particularly of those who are fat. The archetype is the husband who keeps his wife fat, usually because of insecurity or other related reasons. He feels secure because she is so obese that no one else will have her. When his wife tries to lose weight, such a man becomes anxious and tries to get her to go off the diet by tempting her, annoying her, or by otherwise sabotaging her efforts. As she gets close to her weight goal, he becomes more and more anxious and will resort to physical abuse, verbal assaults, and as a last desperate effort may cut off her funds so she cannot continue her weight program. In such cases the majority succomb to the will of the "feeder" partner and stop dieting. For those who stick it out and continue the diet, there is divorce, usually coming on the heels of an increasing amount of abuse.

Not all victims are wives. Many are husbands of insecure

wives or children of insecure parents. There is the case of a massively obese man whose wife constantly nagged him to eat, even while his doctor was present. She was jealous of him, and efforts to get him down to a safe weight were met with tirades and abuse that only ended when he stopped dieting. The woman now has what she wants, a husband so fat and unattractive that no one else would want him.

In summary, you and others who have close contact with the dieter have more influence on him or her than you will ever realize. Without your total assistance and support, the dieter will more than likely fail. The attitude that "food is love" is widespread. The idea that giving food is showing love and refusing food is rejecting love is still too strong for the comfort of most dieters. You can, however, show love in nonfood-related ways—for example, giving a bouquet of flowers on birthdays, Valentine's Day, and other holidays rather than a box of chocolates.

Bibliography

Church, Charles F., and Church, Helen N. *Food Values of Portions Commonly Used*. 12th ed. Philadelphia: J. B. Lippincott Co., 1975.

Cooper, Kenneth H., M.D., M.P.H. *Aerobics*. New York: M. Evans and Co., 1968.

———. *The Aerobics Way*. New York: M. Evans and Co., 1977.

———. *The New Aerobics*. New York: M. Evans and Co., 1970.

Cooper, Kenneth H., M.D., M.P.H., and Cooper, Mildred. *Aerobics for Women*. New York: M. Evans and Co., 1972.

Jones, Jeanne. *The Calculating Cook*. rev. ed. San Francisco: 101 Productions, 1978.

———. *Diet for a Happy Heart*. San Francisco: 101 Productions, 1975.

———. *Fabulous Fiber Cookbook*. San Francisco: 101 Productions, 1977.

———. *Secrets of Salt-Free Cooking*. San Francisco: 101 Productions, 1979.

Kraus, Barbara. *The Dictionary of Sodium, Fats and Cholesterol*. New York: Grosset & Dunlap, 1977.

Leonard, Jon N., Hofer, J. L., and Pritikin, Nathan. *Live Longer*

Now: The First One Hundred Years of Your Life. New York: Grosset & Dunlap, 1974.

Mayer, Jean. M.D. *A Diet for Living.* New York: David McKay Co., 1975.

U.S. Department of Agriculture. *Composition of Foods—Raw, Processed, Prepared.* Revised U.S.D.A. Agricultural Handbook, no. 8., Washington, D.C.: Government Printing Office, 1975.

———. *Nutritive Value of American Foods in Common Units.* U.S.D.A. Agricultural Handbook, no. 456. Washington, D.C.: Government Printing Office, 1975.

Index

Alcoholic beverages, 19-20
  portions, 238-240
Almonds, 195
"Amaretto" Sauce, 198
American Diabetes Association, 13
American Dietetic Association, 13
Apple and Cheese Salad, 94

Baked Salmon, 129
Banana Bread, 164
Banana Breakfast Bullet, 210
Banana soufflé, 184-185
Basic French Dressing, 71
Basic White Cake, 183, 186-187
Bass Buffet Platter, 132-133
Bean sprouts, 122-123
Bechamel Sauce, 64-65
Beef, 148-149, 150-151
  portions, 227, 229, 231
Beef Consommé, 46-47
Beef gravy, 65
Beef Stock, 42-43
Beet Borscht, 53
Bloody Shame, 208

Borscht, 53
Bouillon, 47
Bran, 17
Breads, 16, 220-221
  Banana Bread, 164
  Canyon Ranch Bread, 158-159
  Fat-Free Dill Bread, 160
  Irish Soda Bread, 162
  Lettuce Bread, 163
  Orange Rye Bread, 161
  Pineapple Muffins, 168
  Show-off Popovers, 165
Breakfast bullet, 209-210
Bulgur, 112
Bullet, 35-36, 210
Butter Cookie Crust, 191

C-P-F rations, 11-12
Cabbage, 107-108
Caesar Dressing, 74-75
Caesar Salad, 93-94
Cake, 183, 186-187, 188
Calcutta Consommé, 51
Caloric need, 10-11, 241

Calorie-Cutter's Catsup, 80
Cantonese Sweet-and-Sour Pork, 154-155
Canyon Ranch Bread, 158-159
Carbohydrate-Protein-Fat ratios, 9-10
Carbohydrates, 12-13
Caribbean Rum Sauce, 199-200
Carob Caliente, 205
Carob sauce, 200-202
Carrot cake, 188
Carrot salad, 89
Carrots, 105
Carrots à l'Indienne, 120
Catsup, 80
Cauliflower, 56, 90-91, 96, 108
Cereals, 17
  portions, 221-222
Cheese, 124, 126-127
  portions, 224, 228, 230
Cheese (and apple) salad, 94
Cheese pie, 192-193
Cheese Sauce, 68
Cheese Soufflé, 116-117
Chefs Salad, 99
Chicken, 138-139
  portions, 224, 228
Chicken and snow peas, 141-142
Chicken Curry, 143-144
Chicken Enchilada Torte, 142-143
Chicken gravy, 66
Chicken, pizza, 145-146
Chicken salad, 98-99
Chicken Soup, 58-59
Chicken Stock, 44-45

Chilies, 124
Chinese Chicken and Snow Peas, 141-142
Cholesterol, 8, 21
Choline, 34
Christmas Relish, 85
Cioppino, 136-137
Clams, 136-137
"Coconut" Sauce, 198-199
Cold Banana Soufflé, 184-185
Cold Consommé with Mushrooms, 48
Cold cuts, portions, 230-231
Coleslaw, 88-89
Colorful Coleslaw, 88-89
Compote, 176-177
Confections, 14
Consommé, 46-47, 48, 51
Cookies, 175
Cooper, Kenneth, 9
Cooper's Crispies, 131
Cornish game hens, 146-147
Counterfeit Cocktail, 206
Court Bouillon, 47
Crabs, 136-137
Cracked wheat, 112
Crackers, portions, 223
Creamed Spinach, 106-107
Creamy Cheese Pie, 192-193
Crêpes, 119, 169, 181-182
Crêpes Suzette, 181-182
Crunchy Carob Sauce, 202
Cucumbers, 87
Cuminseed Dressing, 70
Curried Carrot Salad, 89

Curried chicken salad, 98-99
Curried Orange Soup, 58
Curried Yogurt Dressing, 78
Curry, chicken, 143-144

Date Nut Waffles, 171
Defatted drippings, 62-63
Desert Tea, 203-204
Diabetes, 11, 13
Diet Bullet, 35-36
Dieter's Dream Quiche, 126-127
Dieter's Spicy Sausage, 153
Dill bread, 160
Dilled Cucumbers, 87
Dilled Yogurt Dressing, 78-79
Drippings, defatted, 62-63
Duck, portions, 231
Dutch Rum Soufflé, 180-181

Egg Flower Soup, 48-49
Egg Sprout Soup, 49-50
Eggnog, 204
Eggplant Lasagne, 113-114
Eggs, 124-125
    portions, 228
Eggs Foo Yung, 122-123
Emergency Diet, 10, 22, 31-33
Enchilada torte, 142-143
English Pizza, 118
English Trifle, 186-187
Estrogen, 29-30
Exchange method, 9-10, 11-12
Exercise, 9

Fabulous Beef Gravy, 65
Fabulous Chicken Gravy, 66
Fabulous Curried Chicken Salad
    in Lettuce Bowls, 98-99
Fabulous Dressing, 83
Fabulous Fructose Diet, 6-8
    criticisms, 3, 7
Fabulous Fructose Emergency
    Diet, 10, 22, 31-33
Fabulous Fructose Seven-Day
    Maintenance Diet, 21-27
Fabulous Mustard Sauce, 68-69
Fabulous Pilaf, 111
Fabulous Stew, 150-151
Fabulous Turkey Gravy, 67
Fat-Free Dill Bread, 160
Fats, 7, 21-22
    portions, 18, 213, 232-234
"Feeders," 8-9, 246-248, 251
Fettuccine alla Fabulosa, 123
Fettuccine Pasta, 172-173
Fiber, 4, 157
Fish, 129-133
    portions, 225-226
    preparation, 128-129
Fish amandine, 130-131
Fish Stock, 45
Florentine Crêpes, 119
Flour, portions, 222-223
Fluid retention, 29-31
Fondue, 114-115
Frankfurters, 97
French dressing, 71
French toast, 121
Fresh Tomato Soup, 54

Fruit
  fondue, 114-115
  portions, 13-14, 213, 214-216
  soup, 57
Fun 'n Fancy Cookies, 175

Game Hens alla Cacciatora,
  146-147
Game, portions, 225
Garlic-Flavored Oil, 69-70
Gazpacho, 52
German Red Cabbage, 107-108
Glucose-Insulin Trap, 6, 20
Graham-Cracker Piecrust, 194
Gravy, 65-67
Green Goddess Dressing, 79

Ham Slices in Orange Sauce,
  149-150
Hawaiian Carrot Cake, 188
Hawaiian Pineapple Meat Loaf,
  148-149
Herbed Fish Amandine, 130-131
Herbed Vegetable Medley, 104
Herbs, 19
  portions, 236-238
Hot Dog Salad, 97
Huevos Rancheros, 124
Hypoglycemia, 6

Irish Soda Bread, 162
Italian Dressing, 72

Jam, 186-187, 196
Jam omelet, 125
Jamaican Carob Sauce, 201
Jazzy Jelled Water, 176
Jelled water, 176
Jellied Milk, 185-186

Ketosis, 7

Lamb, 152-153
  portions, 227
Lasagne, 113-114
Lavash, 166-167
Lebanese salad, 95
Lecithin, 34
Lemon Bulgur, 112
Lemonade, 206-207
Lettuce Bread, 163
Liquid fructose, 157
Liver Teriyaki, 155-156
Low-Cholesterol Eggnog, 204

Marinated Vegetable Medley, 103
Mashed Potato Spoof, 108
Mayonnaise, 77
Meat loaf, 148-149
Methionine, 34
Milk, jellied, 185-186
Milk, portions, 18-19, 213, 234-236
Minestrone, 60-61
Minted Carrots, 105
Mornay Sauce, 63
Mousse, 178-179

Muffins, 168
Mushrooms, 48
Mustard sauce, 68-69
Mystery Dressing, 82

New England Clams and Vegetables, 137
Nuts, portions, 233-234
Nutty Wild Rice, 109

Oil, garlic flavored, 69-70
Old-Fashioned Lemonade-Stand Lemonade, 206-207
Omelet, 125
Orange Rye Bread, 161
Orange soup, 58
Oysters Rockefeller Casserole, 135

Pancakes, 167
Party Pea Salad, 90
Pasta, 123, 172-173
Pea salad, 90
Peanut Butter Pie, 191-192
Peanut butter, portions, 231
Peanut Butter Punch, 208-209
Perfect Piecrust, 189
pH balance, 39-40
Pie, 190-193
Piecrust, 189, 191, 194
Pilaf, 111
Pineapple meat loaf, 148-149
Pineapple Muffins, 168
Pineapple pie, 190-191

Pizza, 118
Pizza Chicken, 145-146
Popovers, 165
Popular Porridge, 170
Pork, 153-155
    portions, 227, 229, 231
Porridge, 170
Portion method, 9-10, 11-12
Poultry, portions, 224-225, 228
Protein, portions, 17-18, 213, 224-231
Punch, 208-209

Quiche, 126-127

Ramos Fizzle, 207
Raspberry Mousse, 178-179
Ravable Rice, 110
Red cabbage, 107-108
Relish, 85
Rhubarb Compote, 176-177
Rice, 109, 110, 111
Roast Chicken, 138-139
Roast Turkey, 140
Rum sauce, 199-200
Rum soufflé, 180-181
Rye bread, 161

Salad dressings, 70-75, 76-79, 81-83
Salad greens, 84
Salmon, 129, 131
Salt. See Sodium

San Francisco Sourdough French
    Toast, 121
Sauces
    "Amaretto Sauce," 198
    Béchamel Sauce, 64-65
    Caribbean Rum Sauce, 199-200
    Carob Sauce, 200-202
    Cheese Sauce, 68
    "Coconut Sauce," 198-199
    Crunchy Carob Sauce, 202
    Fabulous Mustard Sauce, 68-69
    Jamaican Carob Sauce, 201
    Mornay Sauce, 63
    Tartar Sauce, 75
Sauerkraut, 97
Sauerkraut Salad, 88
Sausage, 153
Scandinavian Fruit Soup, 57
Sea bass, 132-133
Seafood, portions, 225-226
Shashlik, 152-153
Show-off Popovers, 165
Shrimp salad, 96
Shrimps, 136-137
Ski Slope Syndrome, 35
Skinny Dressing, 81
Snapper, 130-131
Snow peas, 141-142
Soda bread, 162
Sodium, 15, 22, 39
Soufflé, 116-117, 180-181, 184-
    185
Soufflé-Textured Tuna Aspic,
    86-87
Soups
    Beet Borscht, 53

Chicken Soup, 58-59
Curried Orange Soup, 58
Egg Flower Soup, 48-49
Egg Sprout Soup, 49-50
Fresh Tomato Soup, 54
Gazpacho, 52
Minestrone, 60-61
Scandinavian Fruit Soup, 57
Split-Pea Soup, 55
Straceiatella alla Romana, 50-51
Strawberry Soup, 61
Vichyssoise Surprise, 56
Sour cream sauce, 179
Sourdough French toast, 121
South Seas Pineapple Pie, 190-191
South Seas Spoof, 90-91
Spiced Almonds, 195
Spices, 19
    portions, 236-238
Spinach, 106-107, 119
Spinach Salad with Walnuts,
    92-93
Split-Pea Soup, 55
Starch, 14-17
Starch, 14-17
    portions, 213, 219-223
Steaming vegetables, 100-103
Stew, 150-151
Stock, 42-47
Straceiatella alla Romana, 50-51
Strawberries Hoffmann-
    La-Roche, 177-178
Strawberry jam, 186-187, 196
Strawberry Jam Omelet, 125
Strawberry Soup, 61
Stress, 30

Striped bass, 132-133
Suppliers, 243-245
Sweet-and-sour pork, 154-155
Swiss Fruit Fondue, 114-115
Syrup (fructose), 14, 34-35
Szechuan Dressing, 76
Szechuan Shrimp Salad, 96

Tabbouli, 95
Tarragon Dressing, 72-73
Tartar Sauce, 75
Tea, 203-204
Toasted Tortilla Triangles, 159
Tomato soup, 54
Trifle, 186-187
Tropical Fruit Smoothie, 209
Tuna, 131
Tuna aspic, 86-87
Tuna in Tartar Sauce, 134
Turkey, 139, 140
    portions, 225
Turkey gravy, 67
Turkey Stock, 43
Turkish Turkey, 139

Veal, portions, 227, 229
Vegetable medley, 103-104
Vegetable, portions, 14-15, 213, 216-220
Vichyssoise Surprise, 56
Vinaigrette Dressing, 73
Vitamin B-complex, 30

Waffles, 171
Waldorf salad, 91-92
Walnuts, 92-93, 98-99
Whipped "cream," 4, 197
White cake, 183
White sauce, 64-65
Wild rice, 109
Wine, 20
    portions, 239
Wonderful Waldorf Salad, 91-92

Yeast, 157
Yogurt, 18-19
Yogurt dressing, 78-79

Zucchini in Herb "Butter," 106